KNIT SHAWLS & WRAPS
in 1 Week

KNIT SHAWLS & WRAPS

in 1 Week

30 Quick Patterns
to Keep You Cozy in Style

Marie Greene

AUTHOR OF *SEAMLESS KNIT SWEATERS IN 2 WEEKS*
AND FOUNDER OF OLIVE KNITS

PAGE STREET
PUBLISHING CO.

PAGE STREET
PUBLISHING CO.

First published in 2019 by

Page Street Publishing Co.

27 Congress Street, Suite 105

Salem, MA 01970

www.pagestreetpublishing.com

Distributed by Macmillan, sales in Canada by The Canadian Manda Group.

23   22   21   20   19   1   2   3   4   5

ISBN-13: 978-1-62414-861-3

ISBN-10: 1-62414-861-1

Library of Congress Control Number: 2019940343

Cover and book design by Rosie Stewart for Page Street Publishing Co.

Photography by Belen Mercer

Printed and bound in the United States

Page Street Publishing protects our planet by donating to nonprofits like The Trustees, which focuses on local land conservation.

FOR MY LITTLE SISTER, *Anna*, THE NEW KNITTER,

WHO RECENTLY SAID THE WORDS "HOLD ON, JUST LET ME FINISH THIS ROW."

NOW YOU UNDERSTAND.

Contents

LAYERING THROUGHOUT THE YEAR

A knitter recently told me that she's been cold since 1963 and that trying to stay warm is the bane of her existence. As one who's spent most of my life turning up the heat and piling on the blankets, I can completely relate to this woman's frustration. And it's for this reason that I think hand knits serve a special—and important—purpose. Sure, they have the potential to add that *je ne sais quoi* to an outfit that needs a kick, but it's more than that.

Growing up in the midwestern part of the United States, I became intimately familiar with the unpredictability of the weather. Sunshine could be misleading. Torrential winds could appear from out of nowhere. And it could snow in the middle of May, for no apparent reason whatsoever. We once had a June hailstorm that totaled half the cars in the neighborhood. You just never know what the weather is going to do, which is why it pays to have a few quick knits you can start *and* finish before a storm hits.

When it comes to wacky weather, it's all about the layers. The trick with layering, though, is that there's a bit of strategy involved. Too many layers can become cumbersome and frustrating, so we have to decide what our layers are meant to do for us. Are we making a fashion statement, or are we trying desperately to stay warm? Or both?

When we're just trying to spice up an outfit, the lighter the layers, the more reasonably we can wear them throughout the year. Mid-weight and lightweight shawls and wraps are a regular part of my wardrobe rotation because they coordinate with just about everything and provide the right amount of warmth without being heavy. Shawls such as Cider Press (page 41) and Puddlejumper (page 107) are airy and easy to wear, and don't take up a lot of space if you get a bit too warm and need to hide them away in your bag.

The heavyweights are for the serious cold—they're for the days when absolutely nothing else will do (see the Glacier Wrap [page 65] or the January Morning Shawl [page 75]). They're dense, cozy and guaranteed to keep you warm, no matter what the weather decides to do.

Most of the shawls and wraps in this book fall somewhere in the middle range for warmth and size, making them quick to knit and versatile to wear. My goal is that you'll be able to find a few new favorites for each season, and will enjoy knitting them in time to wear them.

Designed with efficient stitch patterns and easy-to-memorize repeats (to make them realistic for knitting in about a week), you'll find projects that work well for distracted knitting, last-minute birthdays or holiday knitting and for any project that you'd like to knit quickly without a lot of fuss. I've kept the fiddly bits to a minimum and have aimed for simple—but effective—details to keep the projects interesting without slowing you down. Advanced beginners and intermediate knitters alike will find something accessible on the pages of this book. Use the pattern yardage guidelines to match projects to your schedule and have seasonal shawls and wraps to coordinate with your wardrobe all year long.

Accessories are especially nice for using yarn from your stash, so if you are unable to find the recommended yarn or prefer to use yarn you already have on hand, substitutions are relatively easy to do. I especially love the Flower Girl Shawl (page 101) as a stash-buster, because it calls for three single skeins of yarn in different weights.

Whatever your goal or skill level, I hope you'll find something on these pages to inspire you and keep you cozy throughout the year.

Marie E Greene

Autumn

It will probably come as no surprise that autumn is my favorite season. It's when the air feels rich with change—so palpable you can almost touch it with your fingertips. I love the moment when I finally need a sweater and have to start reaching for extra layers (such as the Applejack Wrap [page 23] or Spiced Ginger Shawl [page 13]) before I leave the house. Autumn is the sweet spot; it's a break from the heat of summer and not yet cold enough to hibernate. It's also my favorite time of year for knitting; there's nothing as inviting as a lapful of wool in the autumn months.

The scent of woodsmoke dancing on the air and the crisp crunch of leaves underfoot make autumn one of the most tactile seasons, inviting us outdoors to experience the transition up close. And don't get me started on the colorworks: the colors in the mountains are nothing short of awe-inspiring.

This tantalizing fall imagery inspired the warm, rustic colors and engaging stitch patterns for the designs in this chapter, and they're perfect for days with variable temperatures. Whether you're dressing up or dressing down, knitting for yourself or for someone else, you'll find a range of mid-weight styles to inspire you.

Spiced Ginger Shawl

A mesmerizing series of faux cables in a rich ginger tweed reminds me of gingerbread dough fresh out of the mixer. You won't need a cable needle for these twists—they're a series of strategic increases and decreases that mimic cables, but without the extra work. Twists and garter stitch team up for an interesting composition of texture and pattern that will keep you engaged from start to finish. The charming bobble bind-off is a nod to frosting buttons on a gingerbread person cookie.

TIMELINE
At a pace of about ½ skein (or about 115 yards [105 m]) per day, you can finish your Spiced Ginger Shawl in about 4 days, with an extra day or so for blocking.

CONSTRUCTION
Knit back and forth (flat) as an asymmetrical piece, this shawl will have you working an increase every right side row to create the shaping. The pattern consists of a repeat of three ginger twists worked throughout, while at the same time building a section of garter stitch that grows with the increases.

SKILL LEVEL
Advanced Beginner

SIZE
One size fits most (see schematic for finished measurements)

MATERIALS

Yarn	• DK weight | The Farmers Daughter Fibers Craggy Tweed | 85% superwash Merino, 15% NEP (tweedy bits) | 231 yards (211 m) per 100 g skein | 2 skeins or 462 yards (422 m) total • Color: Eagle Eye • Yarn substitutions may create different results. Please keep this in mind.
Needles	• U.S. size 8/5 mm (32" [80 cm]) circular needle
Gauge	• 19 st and 26 rows = 4" (10 cm) in pattern stitch, blocked
Notions	• Stitch markers, including a locking marker • Darning needle to weave in ends

STITCH GLOSSARY

[ ]	brackets always indicate a repeat
bet	between
BO	bind off
CO	cast on
dec	decrease
inc	increase
k	knit
kfb	knit into front and back of same st (inc 1)
m	marker
p	purl
pm	place marker
ptbl	purl through the back loop
rep	repeat
RS	right side
sm	slip marker
ssk	slip, slip, knit 2 together (dec 1)
st	stitch/stitches
WS	wrong side
yo	yarn over (inc 1)

SPICED GINGER SHAWL PATTERN

With U.S. size 8/5 mm (32" [80 cm]) circular needle, and using your preferred cast-on method, CO 2 st

ROW 1 (RS): Kfb, k1 (3 st).

ROW 2 (WS): P.

ROW 3 (RS): K1, kfb, k1 (4 st).

TIP: Attach a locking marker anywhere on the front-facing side of row 3 to help keep track of the right side until the pattern begins to form.

ROW 4 (WS): P.

ROW 5 (RS): K1, kfb, k to end (5 st).

ROW 6 (WS): P.

ROW 7 (RS): K1, kfb, k to end (6 st).

ROW 8 (WS): P.

ROW 9 (RS): K1, kfb, k to end (7 st).

ROW 10 (WS): K3, p to end.

REP rows 9 and 10 until you have 37 st, ending after a WS row.

PATTERN ROWS

ROW 1 (RS): K1, kfb, k1, pm, [p1, yo, k3, ssk, k4] rep bet brackets to last 4 st, p1, k3.

ROW 2 (WS): K4, [p9, k1] rep bet brackets to m, sm, k to end.

ROW 3 (RS): K1, kfb, k to m, sm, [p1, k1, yo, k3, ssk, k3] rep bet brackets to last 4 st, p1, k3.

ROW 4 (WS): Rep row 2.

ROW 5 (RS): K1, kfb, k to m, sm, [p1, k2, yo, k3, ssk, k2] rep bet brackets to last 4 st, p1, k3.

ROW 6 (WS): Rep row 2.

ROW 7 (RS): K1, kfb, k to m, sm, [p1, k3, yo, k3, ssk, k1] rep bet brackets to last 4 st, p1, k3.

ROW 8 (WS): Rep row 2.

ROW 9 (RS): K1, kfb, k to m, sm, [p1, k4, yo, k3, ssk] rep bet brackets to last 4 st, p1, k3.

ROW 10 (WS): Rep row 2.

ROW 11 (RS): K1, kfb, k to m, sm, [p1, k9] to last 4 st, p1, k3.

ROW 12 (WS): Rep row 2.

REP Pattern Rows 1–12 until you have 133 st, ending after a WS row.

BOBBLE EDGE BIND-OFF

WORK a bobble in the first stitch as follows: k-yo-k-yo-k into this first st (you have now worked 5 st into the first st). Turn your work to the wrong side and work p1-ptbl-p1-ptbl-p1 into the st you just worked. Turn your work again (to the right side) and k these 5 st. Turn your work again (to the wrong side) and p these 5 st. Turn your work again and k these same 5 st. Now, with the right side facing you and with 5 st on your right needle, insert your left needle into the second st from the tip of the right needle and pass it over the st closest to the tip (binding it off). You should now have 4 st on your right needle. Rep this process again (3 st on your right needle). And again (2 st on your right needle). And one last time (1 st on your right needle). You have now created one bobble.

BO 6 st, then work a bobble as previously instructed.

REP the process above, working a bobble, then binding off 6 st, and repeating this to the end of the row, ending by binding off 5, then working a final bobble as previously instructed.

WEAVE IN the ends and wet block, drawing the points and sides taut on the blocking mat to help draw the shawl into shape and relax the stitches.

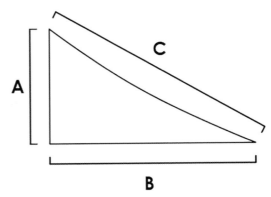

FINISHED MEASUREMENTS

A: 36" (91.5 cm)

B: 56" (142 cm)

C: 60" (152 cm)

Forest Grove Shawl

The first signs of autumn come with the crunch of leaves and the perfume of woodsmoke. For all the virtues of the other seasons, fall is quite possibly the most spectacular in the way it floods the world with a certain familiar ambience. I love the way the air snaps gently against your skin, practically begging for an extra layer of wool. In my nod to autumn, Forest Grove has intriguing (but simple) details that partner eyelets, texture and stripes for a winning combination.

TIMELINE

Designed to be easy to follow and quick on the needles, if you're able to knit through about 100 yards (91 m or roughly ⅓ of a skein) of yarn per day, you can finish at the steady pace of 5 days.

CONSTRUCTION

Beginning at the top center point and worked side to side in a crescent shape with increases on both the right side and wrong side rows (at the edges), your shawl will grow quickly in width without adding bulk to the body. You'll alternate sections of texture with stripes to keep things interesting along the way.

SKILL LEVEL

Intermediate

SIZE

One size fits most (see schematic for finished measurements)

MATERIALS

Yarn	• DK weight | Three Irish Girls Springvale DK | 100% superwash Merino | 270 yards (247 m) per 100 g skein | 500 yards (457 m) total • Color A: Dire Wolf • Color B: Greige is the New Black • Yarn substitutions may create different results. Please keep this in mind.
Needles	• U.S. size 7/4.5 mm (32" [80 cm]) circular needle
Gauge	• 16 st and 20 rows = 4" (10 cm) in stockinette stitch, blocked

MATERIALS

Notions	• Stitch markers • Darning needle to weave in ends
Swatching Tip	• Be sure to knit a striped swatch (and wet block it) so you can test colorfastness before you begin.

STITCH GLOSSARY

[ ]	brackets always indicate a repeat
bet	between
BO	bind off
CO	cast on
inc	increase
k	knit
ktbl	knit through the back loop (this will close up the yo from the previous row)
k-yo-k	knit, yarn over, then knit again into the same st (2 st inc)
m	marker
p	purl
pm	place marker
rem m	remove marker
rep	repeat
RS	right side
sm	slip marker
st	stitch/stitches
WS	wrong side
yo	yarn over (inc 1)

FOREST GROVE PATTERN

With U.S. size 7/4.5 mm (32" [80 cm]) circular needle and Color A, CO 3 st using the cable cast-on method.

NOTE: The cable cast-on method starts your work on the right side immediately.

ROW 1 (RS): [K-yo-k] rep bet brackets 3 times (9 st).

ROW 2 (WS): P1, yo, p to last st, yo, p1 (11 st).

ROW 3 (RS): K1, ktbl, k-yo-k, k5, k-yo-k, ktbl, k1 (15 st).

ROW 4 (WS): P1, yo, p to last st, yo, p1 (17 st).

ROW 5 (RS): K1, ktbl, k-yo-k, k to last 3 st, k-yo-k, ktbl, k1 (21 st).

ROW 6 (WS): Rep row 4 (23 st).

ROW 7 (RS): Rep row 5 (27 st).

ROW 8 (WS): Rep row 4 (29 st).

ROW 9 (RS): Rep row 5 (33 st).

ROW 10 (WS): Rep row 4 (35 st).

ROW 11 (RS): Rep row 5 (39 st).

ROW 12 (WS): Rep row 4 (41 st).

ROW 13 (RS): Rep row 5 (45 st).

ROW 14 (WS): Rep row 4 (47 st).

ROW 15 (RS): Rep row 5 (51 st).

ROW 16 (WS): Rep row 4 (53 st).

ROW 17 (RS): K1, ktbl, k-yo-k, k1, pm, k1, [yo, k3, pass the first of the 3 k st over the other 2 st] rep bet brackets to last 6 st, k1, pm, k2, k-yo-k, ktbl, k1 (57 st).

ROW 18 (WS): P1, yo, p to last st, yo, p1 (59 st).

ROW 19 (RS): K1, ktbl, k-yo-k, k to m, sm, [k3, pass the first of the 3 k st over the other 2 st, yo] rep bet brackets to 2 st before m, rem m, k3, pass the first of the 3 k st over the other 2 st, yo, k to last 3 st, k-yo-k, ktbl, k1 (63 st).

ROW 20 (WS): P1, yo, p to last st, yo, p1 (65 st)—remove markers as you work this row.

NOTE: It is not necessary to cut the yarn when changing colors on the stripes. Simply carry the dormant color up the side as you work, until the pattern indicates otherwise.

WITH COLOR B

ROW 21 (RS): K1, ktbl, k-yo-k, k to last 3 st, k-yo-k, ktbl, k1 (69 st).

ROW 22 (WS): P1, yo, p to last st, yo, p1 (71 st).

WITH COLOR A

ROW 23 (RS): K1, ktbl, k-yo-k, k to last 3 st, k-yo-k, ktbl, k1 (75 st).

ROW 24 (WS): P1, yo, p to last st, yo, p1 (77 st).

WITH COLOR B

ROW 25 (RS): K1, ktbl, k-yo-k, k to last 3 st, k-yo-k, ktbl, k1 (81 st).

ROW 26 (WS): P1, yo, p to last st, yo, p1 (83 st).

WITH COLOR A

ROW 27 (RS): K1, ktbl, k-yo-k, k to last 3 st, k-yo-k, ktbl, k1 (87 st).

ROW 28 (WS): P1, yo, p to last st, yo, p1 (89 st).

ROW 29 (RS): K1, ktbl, k-yo-k, k1, pm, k1, [yo, k3, pass the first of the 3 k st over the other 2 st] rep bet brackets to last 6 st, k1, pm, k2, k-yo-k, ktbl, k1 (93 st).

ROW 30 (WS): P1, yo, p to last st, yo, p1 (95 st).

ROW 31 (RS): K1, ktbl, k-yo-k, k to m, sm, [k3, pass the first of the 3 k st over the other 2 st, yo] rep bet brackets to 2 st before m, rem m, k3, pass the first of the 3 k st over the other 2 st, yo, k to last 3 st, k-yo-k, ktbl, k1 (99 st).

ROW 32 (WS): P1, yo, p to last st, yo, p1 (101 st)—remove the markers as you work this row.

WITH COLOR B
ROW 33 (RS): K1, ktbl, k-yo-k, k to last 3 st, k-yo-k, ktbl, k1 (105 st).

ROW 34 (WS): P1, yo, p to last st, yo, p1 (107 st).

WITH COLOR A
ROW 35 (RS): K1, ktbl, k-yo-k, k to last 3 st, k-yo-k, ktbl, k1 (111 st).

ROW 36 (WS): P1, yo, p to last st, yo, p1 (113 st).

WITH COLOR B
ROW 37 (RS): K1, ktbl, k-yo-k, k to last 3 st, k-yo-k, ktbl, k1 (117 st).

ROW 38 (WS): P1, yo, p to last st, yo, p1 (119 st).

WITH COLOR A
ROW 39 (RS): K1, ktbl, k-yo-k, k to last 3 st, k-yo-k, ktbl, k1 (123 st).

ROW 40 (WS): P1, yo, p to last st, yo, p1 (125 st).

CUT Color B and continue with Color A.

WITH COLOR A
ROW 41 (RS): K1, ktbl, k-yo-k, k1, pm, k1, [yo, k3, pass the first of the 3 k st over the other 2 st] rep bet brackets to last 6 st, k1, pm, k2, k-yo-k, ktbl, k1 (129 st).

ROW 42 (WS): P1, yo, p to last st, yo, p1 (131 st).

ROW 43 (RS): K1, ktbl, k-yo-k, k to m, sm, [k3, pass the first of the 3 k st over the other 2 st, yo] rep bet brackets to 2 st before m, rem m, k3, pass the first of the 3 k st over the other 2 st, yo, k to last 3 st, k-yo-k, ktbl, k1 (135 st).

ROW 44 (WS): P1, yo, p to last st, yo, p1 (137 st)—remove the markers as you work this row.

JOIN Color B.

WITH COLOR B
ROW 45 (RS): K1, ktbl, k-yo-k, k to last 3 st, k-yo-k, ktbl, k1 (141 st).

ROW 46 (WS): P1, yo, p to last st, yo, p1 (143 st).

WITH COLOR A
ROW 47 (RS): K1, ktbl, k-yo-k, k to last 3 st, k-yo-k, ktbl, k1 (147 st).

ROW 48 (WS): P1, yo, p to last st, yo, p1 (149 st).

WITH COLOR B
ROW 49 (RS): K1, ktbl, k-yo-k, k to last 3 st, k-yo-k, ktbl, k1 (153 st).

ROW 50 (WS): P1, yo, p to last st, yo, p1 (155 st).

ROW 56 (WS): P1, yo, p to last st, yo, p1 (173 st)—remove the markers as you work this row.

JOIN Color B.

WITH COLOR B
ROW 57 (RS): K1, ktbl, k-yo-k, k to last 3 st, k-yo-k, ktbl, k1 (177 st).

ROW 58 (WS): P1, yo, p to last st, yo, p1 (179 st).

WITH COLOR A
ROW 59 (RS): K1, ktbl, k-yo-k, k to last 3 st, k-yo-k, ktbl, k1 (183 st).

ROW 60 (WS): P1, yo, p to last st, yo, p1 (185 st).

WITH COLOR B
ROW 61 (RS): K1, ktbl, k-yo-k, k to last 3 st, k-yo-k, ktbl, k1 (189 st).

ROW 62 (WS): P1, yo, p to last st, yo, p1 (191 st).

WITH COLOR A
ROW 63 (RS): K1, ktbl, k-yo-k, k to last 3 st, k-yo-k, ktbl, k1 (195 st).

ROW 64 (WS): P1, yo, p to last st, yo, p1 (197 st).

CUT Color B and continue with Color A.

ROW 65 (RS): K1, ktbl, k-yo-k, k1, pm, k1, [yo, k3, pass the first of the 3 k st over the other 2 st] rep bet brackets to last 6 st, k1, pm, k2, k-yo-k, ktbl, k1 (201 st).

ROW 66 (WS): P1, yo, p to last st, yo, p1 (203 st).

ROW 67 (RS): K1, ktbl, k-yo-k, k to m, sm, [k3, pass the first of the 3 k st over the other 2 st, yo] rep bet brackets to 2 st before m, rem m, k3, pass the first of the 3 k st over the other 2 st, yo, k to last 3 st, k-yo-k, ktbl, k1 (207 st).

ROW 68 (WS): P1, yo, p to last st, yo, p1 (209 st)—remove the markers as you work this row.

JOIN Color B.

WITH COLOR A
ROW 51 (RS): K1, ktbl, k-yo-k, k to last 3 st, k-yo-k, ktbl, k1 (159 st).

ROW 52 (WS): P1, yo, p to last st, yo, p1 (161 st).

CUT Color B and continue with Color A.

WITH COLOR A
ROW 53 (RS): K1, ktbl, k-yo-k, k1, pm, k1, [yo, k3, pass the first of the 3 k st over the other 2 st] rep bet brackets to last 6 st, k1, pm, k2, k-yo-k, ktbl, k1 (165 st).

ROW 54 (WS): P1, yo, p to last st, yo, p1 (167 st).

ROW 55 (RS): K1, ktbl, k-yo-k, k to m, sm, [k3, pass the first of the 3 k st over the other 2 st, yo] rep bet brackets to 2 st before m, rem m, k3, pass the first of the 3 k st over the other 2 st, yo, k to last 3 st, k-yo-k, ktbl, k1 (171 st).

WITH COLOR B

ROW 69 (RS): K1, ktbl, k-yo-k, k to last 3 st, k-yo-k, ktbl, k1 (213 st).

ROW 70 (WS): P1, yo, p to last st, yo, p1 (215 st).

WITH COLOR A

ROW 71 (RS): K1, ktbl, k-yo-k, k to last 3 st, k-yo-k, ktbl, k1 (219 st).

ROW 72 (WS): P1, yo, p to last st, yo, p1 (221 st).

WITH COLOR B

ROW 73 (RS): K1, ktbl, k-yo-k, k to last 3 st, k-yo-k, ktbl, k1 (225 st).

ROW 74 (WS): P1, yo, p to last st, yo, p1 (227 st).

WITH COLOR A

ROW 75 (RS): K1, ktbl, k-yo-k, k to last 3 st, k-yo-k, ktbl, k1 (231 st).

ROW 76 (WS): P1, yo, p to last st, yo, p1 (233 st).

CUT Color B and continue with Color A.

WITH COLOR A

ROW 77 (RS): K1, ktbl, k-yo-k, k1, pm, k1, [yo, k3, pass the first of the 3 k st over the other 2 st] rep bet brackets to last 6 st, k1, pm, k2, k-yo-k, ktbl, k1 (237 st).

ROW 78 (WS): P1, yo, p to last st, yo, p1 (239 st).

ROW 79 (RS): K1, ktbl, k-yo-k, k to m, sm, [k3, pass the first of the 3 k st over the other 2 st, yo] rep bet brackets to 2 st before m, rem m, k3, pass the first of the 3 k st over the other 2 st, yo, k to last 3 st, k-yo-k, ktbl, k1 (243 st).

ROW 80 (WS): P1, yo, p to last st, yo, p1 (245 st)—remove the markers as you work this row.

JOIN Color B.

WITH COLOR B

ROW 81 (RS): K1, ktbl, k-yo-k, k to last 3 st, k-yo-k, ktbl, k1 (249 st).

ROW 82 (WS): P1, yo, p to last st, yo, p1 (251 st).

WITH COLOR A

ROW 83 (RS): K1, ktbl, k-yo-k, k to last 3 st, k-yo-k, ktbl, k1 (255 st).

ROW 84 (WS): P1, yo, p to last st, yo, p1 (257 st).

WITH COLOR B

ROW 85 (RS): K1, ktbl, k-yo-k, k to last 3 st, k-yo-k, ktbl, k1 (261 st).

ROW 86 (WS): P1, yo, p to last st, yo, p1 (263 st).

WITH COLOR A

ROW 87 (RS): K1, ktbl, k-yo-k, k to last 3 st, k-yo-k, ktbl, k1 (267 st).

ROW 88 (WS): P1, yo, p to last st, yo, p1 (269 st).

CUT Color B and continue with Color A.

WITH COLOR A UNTIL OTHERWISE STATED

ROW 89 (RS): K1, ktbl, k-yo-k, k1, pm, k1, [yo, k3, pass the first of the 3 k st over the other 2 st] rep bet brackets to last 6 st, k1, pm, k2, k-yo-k, ktbl, k1 (273 st).

ROW 90 (WS): P1, yo, p to last st, yo, p1 (275 st).

ROW 91 (RS): K1, ktbl, k-yo-k, k to m, sm, [k3, pass the first of the 3 k st over the other 2 st, yo] rep bet brackets to 2 st before m, rem m, k3, pass the first of the 3 k st over the other 2 st, yo, k to last 3 st, k-yo-k, ktbl, k1 (279 st)—remove the markers as you work this row.

ROW 92 (WS): P1, yo, p to last st, yo, p1 (281 st).

ROW 93 (RS): K1, ktbl, k-yo-k, k1, pm, k1, [yo, k3, pass the first of the 3 k st over the other 2 st] rep bet brackets to last 3 st, pm, k1, k-yo-k1, ktbl, k1 (285 st).

ROW 94 (WS): P1, yo, p to last st, yo, p1 (287 st).

ROW 95 (RS): K1, ktbl, k-yo-k, k to m, sm, k1, [yo, k3, pass the first of the 3 k st over the other 2 st] rep bet brackets to 1 st before marker, k1, sm, k to last 3 st, k-yo-k, ktbl, k1 (291 st).

ROW 96 (WS): P1, yo, p to last st, yo, p1 (293 st)—remove markers as you work this row.

CUT Color A and join Color B.

WITH COLOR B

ROW 97 (RS): K1, ktbl, k-yo-k, k to last 3 st, k-yo-k, ktbl, k1 (297 st).

ROW 98 (WS): P1, yo, k* to last st, yo, p1 (299 st). *Note that this is a change from the previous rows, and it is intentional.

ROW 99 (RS): BO in knit with a stretchy or loose bind-off.

FINISHED MEASUREMENTS

A: 61" (155 cm) wide

B: 13½" (34 cm) tall

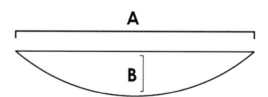

Applejack Wrap

Simple style is my favorite—it's timeless, wearable and makes it easy to leave the house looking like I made an extra effort (even if I didn't). This deliciously large wrap became my second skin the minute it was finished, and I almost can't tear myself away from it. I don't know if it's the rich autumn color, the miles of texture or the airy woolen spun yarn, but this just might be one of my favorite knit things of all time. It just goes to show that it doesn't take a lot of fuss to knit something we'll love forever.

Inspired by chilly autumn evenings and hot cider spiked with applejack brandy, Applejack features steady texture that you can easily knit while you chat; it's perfect for knit nights!

TIMELINE

The airy worsted-spun wool grows quickly on size 8/5 mm needles, and you'll find the pattern requires little fuss once the stitch pattern begins to unfold. I recommend a target goal of knitting 50 grams of yarn per day (or 1 skein of the recommended yarn, which is 50 grams per skein) in order to finish in 6 days. (Although, if you have extra time for knitting, you could easily finish in half that time.)

CONSTRUCTION

Worked from edge to edge to create an asymmetrical triangle, Applejack requires very little extra effort. Keep your edges tidy and you're all set.

SKILL LEVEL

Advanced Beginner

SIZE

One size fits most (see schematic for finished measurements)

MATERIALS

Yarn	• Worsted weight | Brooklyn Tweed Shelter | 100% Targhee-Columbia wool | 140 yards (128 m) per 50 g skein | 5 skeins or 700 yards (640 m) total
	• Color: Wool Socks
	• Yarn substitutions may create different results. Please keep this in mind.

MATERIALS

Needles	• U.S. size 8/5 mm (32" [80 cm]) circular needle
Gauge	• 17 st and 24 rows = 4" (10 cm) in texture pattern (blocked)
Notions	• A locking stitch marker
	• Darning needle to weave in ends

STITCH GLOSSARY

[ ]	brackets always indicate a repeat
bet	between
BO	bind off
CO	cast on
inc	increase
k	knit
kfb	knit into front and back of same st (inc 1)
ktbl	knit through the back loop (twisted st)
p	purl
ptbl	purl through the back loop (twisted st)
rep	repeat
RS	right side
st	stitch/stitches
WS	wrong side

TIP: Although it's incredibly lightweight, Applejack is a generously sized wrap and is meant to bundle around your neck in rich, wooly folds. Feel free to stop sooner (at the conclusion of a repeat) if you'd like to make it a bit smaller.

APPLEJACK WRAP PATTERN

With U.S. size 8/5 mm (32" [80 cm]) circular needle, CO 2 st using the cable cast-on method.

ROW 1 (RS): Kfb, k1 (3 st).

ROW 2 (WS): P.

ROW 3 (RS): K1, kfb, k1 (attach a locking marker anywhere on this side to help keep track of the right side until the pattern is obvious) (4 st).

ROW 4 (WS): P.

ROW 5 (RS): K1, kfb, k to end (5 st).

ROW 6 (WS): P.

ROW 7 (RS): K1, kfb, k to end (6 st).

ROW 8 (WS): P.

ROW 9 (RS): K1, kfb, ktbl, p1, k2 (7 st).

ROW 10 (WS): P3, ptbl, p to end.

ROW 11 (RS): K1, kfb, p1, ktbl, p1, k2 (8 st).

ROW 12 (WS): P3, ptbl, p1, ptbl, p2.

ROW 13 (RS): K1, kfb, [ktbl, p1] twice, k2 (9 st).

ROW 14 (WS): P3, [ptbl, p1] twice, p2.

ROW 15 (RS): K1, kfb, p1, [ktbl, p1] twice, k2 (10 st).

ROW 16 (WS): P3, ptbl, [p1, ptbl] twice, p to end.

ROW 17 (RS): K1, kfb, [ktbl, p1] 3 times, k2 (11 st).

ROW 18 (WS): P3, [ptbl, p1] 3 times, p to end.

ROW 19 (RS): K1, kfb, p1, [ktbl, p1] 3 times, k2 (12 st).

ROW 20 (WS): P3, [ptbl, p1] 3 times, p to end.

ROW 21 (RS): K1, kfb, [ktbl, p1] rep bet brackets to last 2 st, k2 (13 st).

ROW 22 (WS): P3, [ptbl, p1] rep bet brackets to last 2 st, p2.

ROW 23 (RS): K1, kfb, [p1, ktbl] rep bet brackets to last 3 st, k3 (14 st).

ROW 24 (WS): P3, [ptbl, p1] rep bet brackets to last 3 st, ptbl, p2.

REPEAT SERIES

ROW 25 (RS): K1, kfb, [ktbl, p1] rep bet brackets to last 2 st, k2 (15 st).

ROW 26 (WS): P3, [ptbl, p1] rep bet brackets to last 2 st, p2.

ROW 27 (RS): K1, kfb, [p1, ktbl] rep bet brackets to last 3 st, k3 (16 st).

ROW 28 (WS): P3, [ptbl, p1] rep bet brackets to last 3 st, ptbl, p2.

REP rows 25–28 until you have used up nearly all of your yarn (or until desired length). When you have finished the last row of the final repeat, BO on the next row (on the RS) in knit.

WET BLOCK flat, drawing out the sides and edges and pinning them taut.

FINISHED MEASUREMENTS

A: 41" (104 cm) at bind-off edge

B: 63" (160 cm) along bottom edge

C: 74" (188 cm) along the top edge

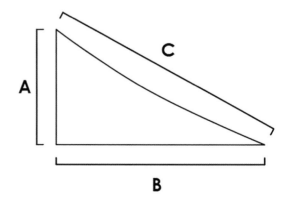

Forager Capelet

Interesting texture and simple ribbing combine in this lovely minimalist shoulder wrap that might classify as something between a shoulder cozy and a poncho. Forager can be worn around the top of the shoulders with rich, deep folds or pulled down over the shoulders as a capelet. If you enjoy the slipped stitch texture, you might consider its sister pattern, the Forager Cowl, on page 135.

TIMELINE

Knit at a loose gauge in aran or heavy worsted weight yarn, Forager can be finished in 6 to 7 days for motivated knitters with an average of 70 to 100 yards (64 to 91 m or about ½ a skein) per day. Because most of the project is worked in stockinette stitch, you'll find this to be ideal for social knitting.

CONSTRUCTION

Worked in the round from the bottom up, the Forager Capelet features clever textural details that catch the eye. The only real focus happens right at the beginning, so you can enjoy long stretches of stockinette for a quick finish. The pattern ends at the neckline with a wide rib.

SKILL LEVEL

Intermediate

SIZE

S/M, M/L, L/XL (see schematic for finished measurements)

MATERIALS

Yarn	• Aran weight | HiKoo Simplinatural | 40% baby alpaca, 40% superfine Merino, 20% mulberry silk | 183 yards (167 m) per 100 g skein | 3 (4, 4) skeins or 500 (600, 700) yards (457 [549, 640] m) total • Color: Slate Grey • Yarn substitutions may create different results. Please keep this in mind.
Needles	• U.S. size 8/5 mm (24-32" [60-80 cm]) circular needle

MATERIALS

Gauge	• 17½ st and 21 rows = 4" (10 cm) in stockinette stitch (blocked)
Notions	• Stitch markers • Darning needle to weave in ends

STITCH GLOSSARY

[ ]	brackets always indicate a repeat
bet	between
BOR	beginning of round
CO	cast on
dec	decrease
k	knit
k2tog	knit 2 st together (dec 1)
kuls	insert right needle under loose strand (from the sl5wyif on the previous row), then knit it with the next st on the left needle, tucking the loose strand in with the st
p	purl
pm	place marker
rep	repeat
sl5wyif	slip 5 st to the right needle with yarn in front (do not knit them)
st	stitch/stitches

FORAGER CAPELET PATTERN

With U.S. size 8/5 mm (24–32" [60–80 cm]) circular needle, CO 200 (240, 280) st using the cable cast-on method. Knit 1 row, then join to work in the round. Pm to denote BOR.

ROUND 1: P2, k5, [p3, k5] rep bet brackets to end of round, p1.

ROUND 2: K2, sl5wyif, [k3, sl5wyif] rep to end, k1.

ROUND 3: Rep round 1.

ROUND 4: K4, kuls, [k7, kuls] rep to end, k3.

REP rounds 1–4 for 5" (13 cm), ending after you've completed round 4.

WORK IN the round in stockinette st (knitting every round) until wrap measures 7 (8, 9)" (18 [20, 23] cm) from cast-on edge.

NEXT ROUND: [K8, k2tog] rep bet brackets to end of round (180, 216, 252 st).

WORK IN the round in stockinette st (knitting every round) until wrap measures 9 (10, 11)" (23 [25, 28] cm) from cast-on edge.

NEXT ROUND: [K7, k2tog] rep bet brackets to end of round (160, 192, 224 st).

WORK IN the round in stockinette st (knitting every round) until wrap measures 11 (12, 13)" (28 [30, 33] cm) from cast-on edge.

NEXT ROUND: [K6, k2tog] rep bet brackets to end of round (140, 168, 196 st).

WORK IN the round in stockinette st (knitting every round) until wrap measures 13 (14, 15)" (33 [36, 38] cm) from cast-on edge.

NEXT ROUND: [K5, k2tog] rep bet brackets to end of round (120, 144, 168 st).

WORK IN the round in stockinette st (knitting every round) until wrap measures 15 (16, 17)" (38 [41, 43] cm) from cast-on edge.

NEXT ROUND: [K4, k2tog] rep bet brackets to end of round (100, 120, 140 st).

NEXT ROUND: [K3, p2] rep bet brackets to end of round.

REP this round until ribbing measures 3" (7.5 cm) and BO in pattern with medium tension.

WEAVE IN ends and wet block flat. Turn as needed for even drying.

FINISHED MEASUREMENTS

A: 23 (27, 32)" (57 [69, 80] cm) at the neck area

B: 46 (55, 64)" (117 [140, 163] cm) at the base

C: 18 (19, 20)" (45 [48, 50] cm)

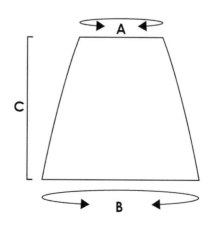

Silver Birch Shawl

Oh, sweet texture. It gets me every time (especially when it's a fun repeat that doesn't require focus). Inspired by the two-toned, textured bark of a silver birch tree, this pretty shawl is a soothing project for your favorite neutrals. I chose natural, undyed wool for this nature-inspired project, but it would be just as lovely with a bold pop of color.

TIMELINE

Silver Birch involves a series of repeating stitches, which means the only real time commitment will come down to how much knitting time you have available. Although not a lightning-fast knit, you can reasonably finish in 7 days by working about 110 yards (101 m or a little less than $\frac{1}{3}$ of a skein) a day.

CONSTRUCTION

Knit flat from the smallest point to the far wide edge (capped with garter stitch on both ends), Silver Birch is worked with two colors in an easy-to-memorize texture that will become second nature after just a few repeats. You'll find the stitch pattern to be quite addictive.

SKILL LEVEL

Advanced Beginner

SIZE

One size fits most (see schematic for finished measurements)

MATERIALS

Yarn	• DK weight | Purl Soho Good Wool | 100% Andean highland wool, undyed | 383 yards (350 m) per 100 g skein | 2 skeins or 766 yards (700 m) total • Color A: Walking Stick (medium brown) 1 skein or 383 yards (350 m)—you will use every yard of Color A • Color B: Winter Grass (off-white) 1 skein or 383 yards (350 m) • Yarn substitutions may create different results. Please keep this in mind.
Needles	• U.S. size 8/5 mm (32" [80 cm]) circular needle

MATERIALS

Gauge	• 26 st and 34 rows = 4" (10 cm) in pattern series (blocked)
Notions	• Locking stitch marker • Darning needle to weave in ends

STITCH GLOSSARY

[ ]	brackets always indicate a repeat
bet	between
BO	bind off
CO	cast on
inc	increase
k	knit
kfb	knit into front and back of same st (inc 1)
rep	repeat
RS	right side
slwyib	slip st with yarn in back (without working it)
slwyif	slip st with yarn in front (without working it)
st	stitch/stitches
WS	wrong side

SILVER BIRCH SHAWL PATTERN

With U.S. size 8/5 mm (32" [80 cm]) circular needle and Color A, CO 2 st using the cable cast-on method (or your preference).

ROW 1 (RS): Kfb, k1 (3 st).

ROW 2 (WS): K.

ROW 3 (RS): K1, kfb, k1 (attach a locking marker anywhere on this side to help keep track of the right side) (4 st).

ROW 4 (WS): K.

ROW 5 (RS): K1, kfb, k to end (5 st).

ROW 6 (WS): K.

REP rows 5 and 6 until you have 23 st.

PATTERN SERIES

ROW 1 (RS): With Color B, k1, kfb, [k1, sl1wyib] rep to last st, k1 (24 st).

ROW 2 (WS): With Color B, k1, [sl1wyif, k1] rep bet brackets to end, k1.

ROW 3 (RS): With Color A, k1, kfb, k to end (25 st).

ROW 4 (WS): With Color A, k to end.

ROW 5 (RS): With Color B, k1, kfb, k1, [k1, sl1wyib] rep bet brackets to last 2 st, k2 (26 st).

ROW 6 (WS): With Color B, k2, [sl1wyif, k1] rep bet brackets to last 2 st, k2.

ROW 7 (RS): With Color A, k1, kfb, k to end (27 st).

ROW 8 (WS): With Color A, k to end.

REP Pattern Series rows 1–8 until you have 186 st, finishing with a WS row.

GARTER EDGE

ROW 1 (RS): With Color A, k1, kfb, k to end.

ROW 2 (WS): With Color A, k to end.

REP these 2 garter rows 5 times in all and bind off on the last row with medium tension (not too loose, not too tight).

WET BLOCK, drawing out the shawl flat on the mat and pinning taut until dry.

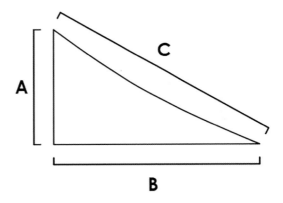

FINISHED MEASUREMENTS

A: 37" (94 cm)

B: 46" (117 cm)

C: 60" (152 cm)

Crackling Fire Wrap

A statement piece doesn't have to be elaborate; the thoughtful partnership of details can turn a simple rectangle into an art piece. With an emphasis on simple stitch movement, Crackling Fire calls for a high-sheen, rayon-blend yarn that—when paired with a vibrant stitch pattern—dances in the light like burning embers. Incredibly simple to knit, this low-maintenance wrap is even easier to wear.

TIMELINE

Knit in a lighter weight yarn, and working through just about 100 yards (91 m or roughly one 50-gram ball of yarn) per day, you can expect this project to take approximately 5 days to finish. However, it requires very little concentration and works well for social knitting.

CONSTRUCTION

Who knew a simple rectangle wrap could hold so much potential? Worked from side to side with tantalizing texture built with simple knits and purls, this pattern uses a row of dramatic decreases followed by a row of dramatic increases to bring the stitch count back to where it began.

SKILL LEVEL

Advanced Beginner

SIZE

One size fits most (see schematic for finished measurements)

MATERIALS

Yarn	• DK weight | Zitron Patina | 55% Merino wool, 45% rayon | 120 yards (110 m) per 50 g ball | 4 balls or 480 yards (439 m) total • Color: Raisin • Yarn substitutions may create different results. Please keep this in mind. • Tip: With so few details to this design, yarn choice can make all the difference in the drape and feel of your finished wrap. The inclusion of rayon in the recommended yarn adds sheen to catch the light and to enhance the stitch pattern. Blends with silk, bamboo or Tencel will work similarly.

MATERIALS

Needles	• U.S. size 6/4 mm (24-32" [60-80 cm]) circular needle
Gauge	• 20 st and 26 rows = 4" (10 cm) in pattern (blocked)
Notions	• Darning needle to weave in ends

STITCH GLOSSARY

[ ]	brackets always indicate a repeat
bet	between
BO	bind off
CO	cast on
dec	decrease
inc	increase
k	knit
k2tog	knit 2 st together (dec 1)
p	purl
p1b	purl 1 st into the horizontal bar between the st on the right needle and the next st on the left needle (inc 1)
rep	repeat
RS	right side
st	stitch/stitches
WS	wrong side

CRACKLING FIRE WRAP PATTERN

With U.S. size 6/4 mm (24-32" [60-80 cm]) circular needle and using the cable cast-on method, CO 80 st.

ROW 1 (RS): K.

ROW 2 (WS): P.

ROW 3 (RS): K2, [k2tog] to last 2 st, k2 (42 st).

ROW 4 (WS): P.

ROW 5 (RS): P2, [p1b, p1] to last 2 st, p2 (80 st).

ROW 6 (WS): P.

ROW 7 (RS): K.

ROW 8 (WS): P.

REP rows 3-8 until you have worked a total of 55 repeats (you will have 55 purl ridges on the RS), then BO in purl on the last row of the final repeat (row 8).

WET BLOCK, pinning flat to ensure the sides are straight and even. Wet blocking will significantly open up the texture and provide additional drape.

FINISHED MEASUREMENTS

A: 16" (41 cm)

B: 51" (130 cm)

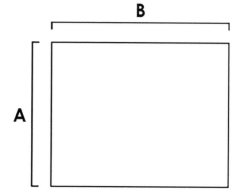

Harvest Moon Wrap

Stripes are always a good idea, but stripes plus tweed? Even better. Harvest Moon features a simple garter stitch with reversible stripes in this sassy mid-weight shawl. A versatile, slightly edgy style with a long crescent shape, Harvest Moon is the perfect accessory for an outfit that just needs a little extra "something." It's not every day that a shawl says, "Wear me with a leather jacket!" but this one seems to.

TIMELINE

The perfect mindless, steady project that you can knit on the go without having to focus, Harvest Moon will go lightning fast. If you can knit approximately 50 grams per day or ½ skein, you can finish this project in 6 days. However, if you have extra knitting time you can easily finish this in 3 to 4 days of social knitting.

CONSTRUCTION

Knit from the top center of the crescent with increases at the edges on both the right and wrong side rows, Harvest Moon grows side to side with a rounded crescent-shape middle.

SKILL LEVEL

Advanced Beginner

SIZE

One size fits most (see schematic for finished measurement)

MATERIALS

Yarn	• DK weight | The Farmers Daughter Fibers Craggy Tweed | 85% superwash Merino, 15% NEP (tweedy bits) | 231 yards (211 m) per 100 g skein | 3 skeins or 693 yards (634 m) total • Color A: Monarch 2 skeins or 462 yards (423 m) • Color B: Paul Newman 1 skein or 231 yards (211 m) • Yarn substitutions may create different results. Please keep this in mind.
Needles	• U.S. size 8/5 mm (32" [80 cm]) circular needle

MATERIALS

Gauge	• 16 st and 34 rows = 4" (10 cm) in garter stitch (blocked)
Notions	• Darning needle to weave in ends
Swatching Tip	• Knit your swatch in both colors and wet block to check colorfastness.

STITCH GLOSSARY

[ ]	brackets always indicate a repeat
BO	bind off
CO	cast on
inc	increase
k	knit
ktbl	knit through the back loop (this will close up the yo from the previous row)
k-yo-k	knit, yarn over, then knit again into the same st (2 st inc)
p	purl
rep	repeat
RS	right side
st	stitch/stitches
WS	wrong side
yo	yarn over (inc 1)

HARVEST MOON WRAP PATTERN

With U.S. size 8/5 mm (32" [80 cm]) circular needle and Color A (pink), CO 3 st using the cable cast-on method.

NOTE: The cable cast-on method starts your work on the right side immediately.

ROW 1 (RS): [K-yo-k] 3 times (9 st).

ROW 2 (WS): P1, yo, k to last st, yo, p1 (11 st).

ROW 3 (RS): K1, ktbl, k-yo-k, k5, k-yo-k, ktbl, k1 (15 st).

ROW 4 (WS): P1, yo, k to last st, yo, p1 (17 st).

ROW 5 (RS): K1, ktbl, k-yo-k, k to last 3 st, k-yo-k, ktbl, k1 (21 st).

ROW 6 (WS): Rep row 4 (23 st).

ROW 7 (RS): Rep row 5 (27 st).

ROW 8 (WS): Rep row 4 (29 st).

ROW 9 (RS): Rep row 5 (33 st).

ROW 10 (WS): Rep row 4 (35 st).

ROW 11 (RS): Rep row 5 (39 st).

ROW 12 (WS): Rep row 4 (41 st).

ROW 13 (RS): Rep row 5 (45 st).

ROW 14 (WS): Rep row 4 (47 st).

ROW 15 (RS): Rep row 5 (51 st).

ROW 16 (WS): Rep row 4 (53 st).

ROW 17 (RS): Rep row 5 (57 st).

ROW 18 (WS): Rep row 4 (59 st).

ROW 19 (RS): Rep row 5 (63 st)—cut Color A.

WITH COLOR B (GREY)

ROW 20 (WS): Rep row 4 (65 st).

ROW 21 (RS): Rep row 5 (69 st).

ROW 22 (WS): Rep row 4 (71 st).

ROW 23 (RS): Rep row 5 (75 st).

ROW 24 (WS): Rep row 4 (77 st)—cut Color B.

WITH COLOR A (PINK)

ROW 25 (RS): Rep row 5 (81 st).

ROW 26 (WS): Rep row 4 (83 st).

ROW 27 (RS): Rep row 5 (87 st).

ROW 28 (WS): Rep row 4 (89 st).

ROW 29 (RS): Rep row 5 (93 st).

ROW 30 (WS): Rep row 4 (95 st).

ROW 31 (RS): Rep row 5 (99 st).

ROW 32 (WS): Rep row 4 (101 st).

ROW 33 (RS): Rep row 5 (105 st).

ROW 34 (WS): Rep row 4 (107 st).

ROW 35 (RS): Rep row 5 (111 st).

ROW 36 (WS): Rep row 4 (113 st).

ROW 37 (RS): Rep row 5 (117 st).

ROW 38 (WS): Rep row 4 (119 st).

ROW 39 (RS): Rep row 5 (123 st)—cut Color A.

REP rows 20–39 (alternating colors as directed). Continue increasing 4 st every RS row and increasing 2 st every WS row as established until you have used nearly all the available yarn.

BO on a RS row in knit with loose tension in a Color A section.

WET BLOCK, pinning the top edge flat (and taut) along the blocking mat. Draw out the crescent curve and pin into shape. Let dry.

FINISHED MEASUREMENTS

A: 81" (206 cm) wide

B: 13½" (34 cm) tall

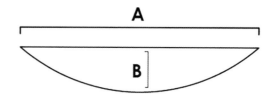

Cider Press Shawl

I never trust the weather report. No matter how favorable the forecast might be, I like to take a little something warm with me—just in case. There's nothing worse than leaving the house in short sleeves and realizing (too late) that you needed more. I chose a traditional "feather and fan" lacework and paired it with tweedy superwash wool for a contemporary mash-up of old and new styles. Cider Press is knit at a relatively loose gauge to create an airy, lightweight fabric, making it perfect for those early autumn months when the weather can't make up its mind.

TIMELINE
The easy repetition and intuitive lacework (not to mention the larger gauge) make Cider Press the ideal quick knit for a long weekend. At a pace of about 1 skein (or roughly 231 yards [211 m]) a day, you can finish in about 3 days (or take your time and savor it during the course of the week).

CONSTRUCTION
Knit side to side from the smallest point to the longest wave panel, Cider Press is worked with staggered increases along one edge. The result is a shape somewhere between an elongated triangle and a boomerang. The placement of the lace extends the shape and adds visual interest and drape.

SKILL LEVEL
Advanced Beginner

SIZE
One size fits most (see schematic for finished measurements)

MATERIALS

Yarn	• DK weight | The Farmers Daughter Fibers Craggy Tweed | 85% superwash Merino, 15% NEP (tweedy bits) | 231 yards (211 m) per 100 g skein | 2 skeins or 462–480 yards (422–439 m) total*
	• Color: Monarch
	• *The original sample was knit with exactly 2 skeins of yarn—462 yards (422 m)—but because yardage can vary between skeins (with any yarn) and any variations in your stitch or row gauge can affect yarn usage, you may need a few additional yards to complete your project.
	• Yarn substitutions may create different results. Please keep this in mind.
Needles	• U.S. size 8/5 mm (32" [80 cm]) circular needle
Gauge	• 16½ st and 22 rows = 4" (10 cm) in stockinette stitch, blocked
Notions	• Stitch markers, including a locking marker • Darning needle to weave in ends

STITCH GLOSSARY

[ ]	brackets always indicate a repeat
BO	bind off
CO	cast on
dec	decrease
inc	increase
k	knit
k2tog	knit 2 st together (dec 1)

(continued)

STITCH GLOSSARY

kfb	knit into front and back of same st (inc 1)
m	marker
p	purl
pm	place marker
rep	repeat
RS	right side
sm	slip marker
st	stitch/stitches
WS	wrong side
yo	yarn over (inc 1)

CIDER PRESS SHAWL PATTERN

With U.S. size 8/5 mm (32" [80 cm]) circular needle, and using your preferred cast-on method, CO 2 st.

ROW 1 (RS): Kfb, k1.

ROW 2 (WS): P.

ROW 3 (RS): K1, kfb, k1 (attach a locking marker anywhere on this side to help keep track of the right side).

ROW 4 (WS): P.

ROW 5 (RS): K1, kfb, k to end.

ROW 6 (WS): P.

REP rows 5 and 6 until you have 23 st. On the last WS row, knit instead of purl.

NEXT ROW (RS): K1, kfb, pm, [k2tog] 3 times, *[yo, k1] 6 times, [k2tog] 3 times, rep from * to last 3 st, pm, k3.

NEXT ROW (WS): K.

NEXT ROW (RS): K1, kfb, k to m, sm, [k2tog] 3 times, *[yo, k1] 6 times, [k2tog] 3 times, rep from * to m, sm, k3.

NEXT ROW (WS): K.

NEXT ROW (RS): K1, kfb, k to m, sm, [k2tog] 3 times, *[yo, k1] 6 times, [k2tog] 3 times, rep from * to m, sm, k3.

NEXT ROW (WS): K.

NEXT ROW (RS): K1, kfb, k to m, sm, [k2tog] 3 times, *[yo, k1] 6 times, [k2tog] 3 times, rep from * to m, sm, k3.

NEXT ROW (WS): K.

NEXT ROW (RS): K1, kfb, k to m, sm, [k2tog] 3 times, *[yo, k1] 6 times, [k2tog] 3 times, rep from * to m, sm, k3.

NEXT ROW (WS): K.

NEXT ROW (RS): K1, kfb, k to end.

NEXT ROW (WS): P.

REP these 2 rows until you have 41 st, ending with the RS row (don't work the last WS row of the repeat).

TIP: As soon as you have 20 stitches before the first marker, it's time to begin another lace pattern. This will save you time from having to count all the stitches to check your place—the stitches between the previous markers should not change count and will always be a multiple of 18. When you've reached 20 stitches at the start of the row before the first marker, place a new marker at the start of the row as described and remove the previous marker when you get to it.

KNIT the next WS row, then:

NEXT ROW (RS): K1, kfb, pm, *[k2tog] 3 times, [yo, k1] 6 times, [k2tog] 3 times, rep from * to last 3 st, pm, k3.

NEXT ROW (WS): K.

REP these 2 rows 4 times more (for a total of 5).

NEXT ROW (RS): K1, kfb, k to end.

NEXT ROW (WS): P.

REP these 2 rows until you have 59 st, ending after a RS row.

NEXT ROW (WS): K.

NEXT ROW (RS): K1, kfb, pm, *[k2tog] 3 times, [yo, k1] 6 times, [k2tog] 3 times, rep from * to last 3 st, pm, k3.

NEXT ROW (WS): K.

REP these 2 rows 4 times more (for a total of 5).

NEXT ROW (RS): K1, kfb, k to end.

NEXT ROW (WS): P.

REP these 2 rows until you have 77 st, ending after a RS row.

NEXT ROW (WS): K.

NEXT ROW (RS): K1, kfb, pm, *[k2tog] 3 times, [yo, k1] 6 times, [k2tog] 3 times, rep from * to last 3 st, pm, k3.

NEXT ROW (WS): K.

REP these 2 rows 4 times more (for a total of 5).

NEXT ROW (RS): K1, kfb, k to end.

NEXT ROW (WS): P.

REP these 2 rows until you have 95 st, ending after a RS row.

NEXT ROW (WS): K.

NEXT ROW (RS): K1, kfb, pm, *[k2tog] 3 times, [yo, k1] 6 times, [k2tog] 3 times, rep from * to last 3 st, pm, k3.

NEXT ROW (WS): K.

REP these 2 rows 4 times more (for a total of 5).

NEXT ROW (RS): K1, kfb, k to end.

NEXT ROW (WS): P.

REP these 2 rows until you have 113 st, ending after a RS row.

NEXT ROW (WS): K.

NEXT ROW (RS): K1, kfb, pm, *[k2tog] 3 times, [yo, k1] 6 times, [k2tog] 3 times, rep from * to last 3 st, pm, k3.

NEXT ROW (WS): K.

REP these 2 rows 4 times more (for a total of 5).

NEXT ROW (RS): K1, kfb, k to end.

NEXT ROW (WS): P.

REP these 2 rows until you have 131 st, ending after a RS row.

NEXT ROW (WS): K.

NEXT ROW (RS): K1, kfb, pm, *[k2tog] 3 times, [yo, k1] 6 times, [k2tog] 3 times, rep from * to last 3 st, pm, k3.

NEXT ROW (WS): K.

REP these 2 rows 4 times more (for a total of 5).

At the conclusion of the final (seventh) lace repeat, knit a RS row, removing markers as you go, then BO on the WS row in k with medium loose tension.

WET BLOCK and pin flat, drawing out the lace panels and edges so they are taut until dry.

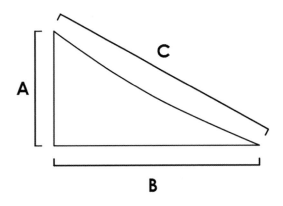

FINISHED MEASUREMENTS

A: 38" (97 cm)

B: 46" (117 cm)

C: 53" (135 cm)

Winter

If there were no other reason to be a knitter, the bone-chilling months of winter would be enough. It's as if we've trained all year for this moment, and now—when the temperature drops and the first snow falls—we're ready and waiting. And although I know it arrives on schedule every year, sometimes winter sneaks up on me. That's why I'm always grateful for a stash of wool and needles at the ready for a quick knit, such as the shawls and wraps in this chapter—just in time for the change of season.

Last year we had a colder winter than usual, and I admit I had gotten a bit lazy with keeping track of my warm winter things. They were packed away (somewhere) and I hadn't really needed them in a while. So when our winter weather grew colder and colder still, I realized it was time to get serious about my woolies. I couldn't find a single hat or mitten in my entire house (how does that even happen?).

What saved me, though, were my shawls. Even with only a light jacket, the right kind of wrap can double your warmth on a cold day. Fallen Petals (page 77) and Sugarplum (page 69) became my go-to shawls this past winter, especially during travel to areas that were much snowier than what I'm used to.

The shawls and wraps in this chapter were designed with extra warmth in mind. The Glacier Wrap on page 65 is the ultimate in dense coziness, without being too bulky to wear. Whether you're in a moderate climate and only need a little something extra, or you're like me and need layers no matter where you live, you'll find toasty, wooly wraps and shawls to get you through the winter months.

Winter Solstice Wrap

I love the impact of a dramatic stitch pattern; it can turn a simple piece into a statement. Winter Solstice is stunning in its simplicity, but features graphic horizontal bands of texture that invite the eye. Knitters and non-knitters alike will be intrigued by the composition of the stitch and how it's created. (There's no need to tell them how simple it really is—that can be our little secret.)

TIMELINE

The combination of soft, delightful wool and a compelling stitch pattern will keep you eager to work on this project, which can easily be finished in about 6 days by working through a bit less than 100 yards (91 m or roughly ½ a skein) of yarn per day.

CONSTRUCTION

A top-down shoulder cozy worked in the round, Winter Solstice features elongated stitches that are created by wrapping the yarn around the needle multiple times. These stitches are twisted and knit together to create bold ridges of texture.

SKILL LEVEL

Intermediate

SIZE

One size fits most (see schematic for finished measurements)

MATERIALS

Yarn	• Aran weight | HiKoo Oh! | 100% super baby alpaca | 191 yards (175 m) per 100 g skein | 3 skeins or 573 yards (524 m) total
	• Color: Heavens
	• Yarn substitutions may create different results. Please keep this in mind.
Needles	• U.S. size 7/4.5 mm (16" [40 cm]) circular needle (neck)
	• U.S. size 9/5.5 mm (24 and 32" [60 and 80 cm]) circular needles (body)
Gauge	• 19 st and 24 rows = 4" (10 cm) in stockinette stitch (blocked)
Notions	• Stitch markers
	• Darning needle to weave in ends

STITCH GLOSSARY

[ ]	brackets always indicate a repeat
bet	between
BO	bind off
BOR	beginning of row
CO	cast on
inc	increase
k	knit
kfb	knit into front and back of same st (inc 1)
p	purl
pm	place marker
rep	repeat
sl	slip
st	stitch/stitches
yo	yarn over (inc 1)

WINTER SOLSTICE WRAP PATTERN

With U.S. size 7/4.5 mm (16" [40 cm]) circular needle CO 120 st.

FOUNDATION ROW: [K2, p2] to end of row, join to work in the round. Pm to denote BOR.

RIBBING ROUND: [K2, p2] to end of round.

REP the Ribbing Round until your ribbed neckline measures 2" (5 cm) from cast-on edge.

NEXT ROUND: [K3, kfb] to end of round (150 st).

TRANSITION to U.S. size 9/5.5 mm (24" [60 cm]) circular needle as you work the next round.

KNIT 5 rounds.

NEXT ROUND: P.

NEXT ROUND: [K1, winding yarn around needle 3 times] rep to end of round.

NEXT ROUND: [Sl5 st purlwise to the right needle without working them, dropping the loops in the process. Slide these 5 st back to the left needle and work the next step into all 5 loops together at once as if a single st as follows: k1, yo, k1, yo, k1.] Rep bet brackets to end (no st inc).

NEXT ROUND: P.

WORK IN stockinette st (knitting every round) for 2" (5 cm).

INCREASE ROUND: [K9, kfb] rep to end of round (165 st).

NEXT ROUND: P.

NEXT ROUND: [K1, winding yarn around needle 3 times] rep to end of round.

NEXT ROUND: [Sl5 st purlwise to the right needle without working them, dropping the loops in the process. Slide these 5 st back to left needle and work the next step into all 5 loops together at once as if a single st as follows: k1, yo, k1, yo, k1.] Rep bet brackets to end, ending p1 (no st inc).

NEXT ROUND: P.

WORK IN stockinette st (knitting every round) for 2" (5 cm).

INCREASE ROUND: [K10, kfb] rep to end of round (180 st).

NEXT ROUND: P.

NEXT ROUND: [K1, winding yarn around needle 3 times] rep to end of round.

NEXT ROUND: [Sl5 st purlwise to the right needle without working them, dropping the loops in the process. Slide these 5 st back to the left needle and work the next step into all 5 loops together at once as if a single st as follows: k1, yo, k1, yo, k1.] Rep bet brackets to end (no st inc).

NEXT ROUND: P.

WORK IN stockinette st (knitting every round) for 2" (5 cm).

INCREASE ROUND: [K5, kfb] rep to end of round (210 st).

NEXT ROUND: P.

NEXT ROUND: [K1, winding yarn around needle 3 times] rep to end of round.

NEXT ROUND: [Sl5 st purlwise to the right needle without working them, dropping the loops in the process. Slide these 5 st back to the left needle and work the next step into all 5 loops together at once as if a single st as follows: k1, yo, k1, yo, k1.] Rep bet brackets to end (no st inc).

NEXT ROUND: P.

WORK IN stockinette st (knitting every round) for 2" (5 cm).

INCREASE ROUND: [K6, kfb] rep to end of round (240 st).

NEXT ROUND: P.

NEXT ROUND: [K1, winding yarn around needle 3 times] rep to end of round.

NEXT ROUND: [Sl5 st purlwise to the right needle without working them, dropping the loops in the process. Slide these 5 st back to the left needle and work the next step into all 5 loops together at once as if a single st as follows: k1, yo, k1, yo, k1.] Rep bet brackets to end (no st inc).

NEXT ROUND: P.

WORK IN the round in stockinette st for 2" (5 cm). Transition to [k2, p2] ribbing (rep bet brackets) until ribbing measures 1¼" (3 cm). BO in pattern with medium tension.

WET BLOCK flat until dry.

FINISHED MEASUREMENTS

A: 25" (63 cm) neck

B: 51" (130 cm) base

C: 20" (51 cm) top to bottom

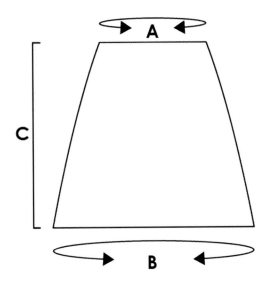

Snow Day Shawl

Growing up in the midwestern part of the United States, we were a bit hardened to the challenges of winter weather. Snow days from school were few and far between; our district didn't call off school unless our very lives were in peril (and even then, it sure seemed like they took their time thinking about it). My Snow Day Shawl is an homage to those blessed days when the weather gave us plump flakes of snow, freezing rain, hail, flurries and maybe even sheets of ice (or any combination thereof) so we could stay home from school. You'll see these weather patterns mimicked throughout the stitches on this nostalgic shawl. It's incredibly cozy and warm, and just the right size to wrap once and pin closed—bulky, but in a manageable size.

TIMELINE

Knit in a super bulky yarn on large needles, the primary time commitment to this shawl will be your comfort level working with heavier yarn. (I have found that knitters often work a bit more slowly with bulky yarn.) Knitting at a rate of approximately 50 yards (46 m, about $^2/_3$ skein or about 46 grams) per day, you can easily finish in about 5 days.

CONSTRUCTION

Snow Day is a triangle shawl worked from the bottom center point to the top with a series of increases at the edges.

SKILL LEVEL

Intermediate

SIZE

One size fits most (see schematic for finished measurements)

MATERIALS

Yarn
- Super bulky weight | Lolodidit Lo Biggity | 80% superwash Merino, 20% nylon | 75 yards (69 m) per 100 g skein | 4 skeins or 300 yards (274 m) total
- Color: Yeti
- Yarn substitutions may create different results. Please keep this in mind.

Needles
- U.S. size 10/6 mm (32" [80 cm]) circular needle

MATERIALS

Gauge
- 13 st and 20 rows = 4" (10 cm) in stockinette stitch (blocked)

Notions
- Stitch markers
- Darning needle to weave in ends

STITCH GLOSSARY

[ ]	brackets always indicate a repeat
bet	between
BO	bind off
CO	cast on
dec	decrease
inc	increase
k	knit
k2tog	knit 2 st together (dec 1)
m	marker
p	purl
pm	place marker
psso	pass slipped st over
p2sso	pass 2 slipped st over
rep	repeat
RS	right side

(continued)

STITCH GLOSSARY

sl1	slip 1 st
sl2	slip 2 st
sm	slip marker
st	stitch/stitches
WS	wrong side
yo	yarn over (inc 1)

SNOW DAY SHAWL PATTERN

With U.S. size 10/6 mm (32" [80 cm]) circular needle, CO 3 st using the cable cast-on method.

NOTE: When slipped stitches are indicated, they will always be slipped as if to knit.

ROW 1 (RS): K, yo, k1, yo, k1 (5 st).

ROW 2 (WS): P.

ROW 3 (RS): K1, yo, k to 1 st before end, yo, k1.

REP rows 2 and 3 until you have 13 st, ending with a WS row.

NEXT ROW (RS): K, yo, k to 1 st before end, yo, k1 (15 st).

NEXT ROW (WS): K1, [p1, k1] to end.

REP these 2 rows 4 times more (23 st).

NEXT ROW (RS): K1, yo, k to 1 st before end, yo, k1 (25 st).

NEXT ROW (WS): P.

START SNOWFLAKE LACE

NEXT ROW (RS): K1, yo, pm, k5, sl1, k1, psso, yo, k1, yo, k2tog, k3, sl1, k1, psso, yo, k1, yo, k2tog, k5, pm, yo, k1 (27 st).

NEXT ROW (WS): P.

NEXT ROW (RS): K1, yo, k1, sm, k6, yo, sl2, k1, p2sso, yo, k5, yo, sl2, k1, p2sso, yo, k6, sm, k1, yo, k1 (29 st).

NEXT ROW (WS): P.

NEXT ROW (RS): K1, yo, k to m, sm, k5, sl1, k1, psso, yo, k1, yo, k2tog, k3, sl1, k1, psso, yo, k1, yo, k2tog, k5, sm, k to last st, yo, k1 (31 st).

NEXT ROW (WS): P.

NEXT ROW (RS): K1, yo, k to m, sm, k1, sl1, k1, psso, yo, k1, yo, k2tog, [k3, sl1, k1, psso, yo, k1, yo, k2tog] rep bet brackets once more, k1, sm, k to last st, yo, k1 (33 st).

NEXT ROW (WS): P.

NEXT ROW (RS): K1, yo, k to m, sm, k2, yo, sl2, k1, p2sso, yo, [k5, yo, sl2, k1, p2sso, yo] rep bet brackets once more, k2, sm, k to last st, yo, k1 (35 st).

NEXT ROW (WS): P.

NEXT ROW (RS): K1, yo, k to m, sm, k1, sl1, k1, psso, yo, k1, yo, k2tog, [k3, sl1, k1, psso, yo, k1, yo, k2tog] rep bet brackets once more, k1, sm, k to last st, yo, k1 (37 st).

NEXT ROW (WS): P.

NEXT ROW (RS): K1, yo, k to m, sm, k5, sl1, k1, psso, yo, k1, yo, k2tog, k3, sl1, k1, psso, yo, k1, yo, k2tog, k5, sm, k to last st, yo, k1 (39 st).

NEXT ROW (WS): P.

NEXT ROW (RS): K1, yo, k to m, sm, k6, yo, sl2, k1, p2sso, yo, k5, yo, sl2, k1, p2sso, yo, k6, sm, k to last st, yo, k1 (41 st).

NEXT ROW (WS): P.

NEXT ROW (RS): K1, yo, k to m, sm, k5, sl1, k1, psso, yo, k1, yo, k2tog, k3, sl1, k1, psso, yo, k1, yo, k2tog, k5, sm, k to last st, yo, k1 (43 st).

NEXT ROW (WS): P—remove markers on this row.

NEXT ROW (RS): K1, yo, k to 1 st before end, yo, k1 (45 st).

NEXT ROW (WS): K1, [p1, k1] rep to end.

REP these 2 rows 4 times more (53 st).

NEXT ROW (RS): K1, yo, k to 1 st before end, yo, k1 (55 st).

NEXT ROW (WS): P.

SNOWFLAKE LACE (SECOND REPEAT)

NEXT ROW (RS): K1, yo, pm, k4, sl1, k1, psso, yo, k1, yo, k2tog, [k3, sl1, k1, psso, yo, k1, yo, k2tog] rep bet brackets to 5 st before end, k4, pm, yo, k1 (57 st).

NEXT ROW (WS): P.

NEXT ROW (RS): K1, yo, k1, sm, k5, yo, sl2, k1, p2sso, yo, [k5, yo, sl2, k1, p2sso, yo] rep bet brackets to last 7 st, k5, sm, k1, yo, k1 (59 st).

NEXT ROW (WS): P.

NEXT ROW (RS): K1, yo, k to m, sm, k4, sl1, k1, psso, yo, k1, yo, k2tog, [k3, sl1, k1, psso, yo, k1, yo, k2tog] rep bet brackets to 4 st before m, k4, sm, k to last st, yo, k1 (61 st).

NEXT ROW (WS): P.

NEXT ROW (RS): K1, yo, k to m, sm, sl1, k1, psso, yo, k1, yo, k2tog, [k3, sl1, k1, psso, yo, k1, yo, k2tog] rep bet brackets to m, sm, k to last st, yo, k1 (63 st).

NEXT ROW (WS): P.

NEXT ROW (RS): K1, yo, k to m, sm, k1, yo, sl2, k1, p2sso, yo, [k5, yo, sl2, k1, p2sso, yo] rep bet brackets to 1 st before m, k1, sm, k to last st, yo, k1 (65 st).

NEXT ROW (WS): P.

NEXT ROW (RS): K1, yo, k to m, sm, sl1, k1, psso, yo, k1, yo, k2tog, [k3, sl1, k1, psso, yo, k1, yo, k2tog] rep bet brackets once more, sm, k to last st, yo, k1 (67 st).

NEXT ROW (WS): P.

NEXT ROW (RS): K1, yo, k to m, sm, k4, sl1, k1, psso, yo, k1, yo, k2tog, [k3, sl1, k1, psso, yo, k1, yo, k2tog] rep bet brackets to 4 st before m, k4, sm, k to last st, yo, k1 (69 st).

NEXT ROW (WS): P.

NEXT ROW (RS): K1, yo, k to m, sm, k5, [yo, sl2, k1, p2sso, yo, k5] rep bet brackets to m, sm, k to last st, yo, k1 (71 st).

NEXT ROW (WS): P.

NEXT ROW (RS): K1, yo, k to m, sm, k4, sl1, k1, psso, yo, k1, yo, k2tog, [k3, sl1, k1, psso, yo, k1, yo, k2tog] rep bet brackets to last 4 st before m, k4, sm, k to last st, yo, k1 (73 st).

NEXT ROW (WS): P—remove markers as you work this row.

SEED STITCH

NEXT ROW (RS): K1, yo, k to 1 st before end, yo, k1 (75 st).

NEXT ROW (WS): K1, [p1, k1] rep to end.

REP these 2 rows 4 times more (83 st).

NEXT ROW (RS): K1, yo, k to 1 st before end, yo, k1 (85 st).

NEXT ROW (WS): P.

STOCKINETTE

NEXT ROW (RS): K1, yo, k to 1 st before end, yo, k1 (87 st).

NEXT ROW (WS): P.

REP these 2 rows 7 times more (101 st).

SEED STITCH

NEXT ROW (RS): K1, yo, k to 1 st before end, yo, k1 (103 st).

NEXT ROW (WS): K1, [p1, k1] rep to end.

REP these 2 rows 4 times more (111 st).

NEXT ROW (RS): K1, yo, k to 1 st before end, yo, k1 (113 st).

NEXT ROW (WS): P.

EYELET ZAG

NEXT ROW (RS): K1, yo, k1, [yo, k2tog] rep bet brackets to last st, yo, k1 (115 st).

NEXT ROW (WS): P.

REP these 2 rows until you have 119 st.

SEED STITCH FINISH

NEXT ROW (RS): K1, yo, k to 1 st before end, yo, k1 (121 st).

NEXT ROW (WS): K1, [p1, k1] rep to end.

REP these 2 rows 4 times more (129 st).

NEXT ROW (RS): BO in k with medium loose tension.

WET BLOCK flat, pinning the shawl taut to draw out the eyelets and snowflakes and to ensure your edges are straight.

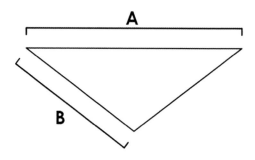

FINISHED MEASUREMENTS

A: 45" (114 cm) tip to tip

B: 33" (84 cm) cast-on to wingtip

Early Frost Shawl

Winter in the Pacific Northwest is characterized by moody grey skies and rain with the occasional frosty morning. I love having warm layers that are as perfect with my pajamas and morning coffee as they are for an evening out on the town with my husband. This simple, steady shawl with its soft, ruched waves has a quiet elegance about it. Its pattern is subtle enough that it can work easily with whatever you happen to be wearing.

TIMELINE

Most of the knitting time is spent working in stockinette stitch, which means this project is perfect for social knitting. Knitting approximately ½ of a 100-gram skein of yarn each day (or about 116 yards [106 m]), motivated knitters can easily finish Early Frost in about 6 days.

CONSTRUCTION

Knit side to side from the smallest point to the far flat edge (where the slight ruffle sits), Early Frost is worked with staggered increases along one edge. The result is an elongated triangle with ruched panels worked in repetition.

SKILL LEVEL

Advanced Beginner

SIZE

One size fits most (see schematic for finished measurements)

MATERIALS

Yarn	• DK weight | The Farmers Daughter Fibers Craggy Tweed | 85% superwash Merino, 15% NEP (tweedy bits) | 231 yards (211 m) per 100 g skein | 3 skeins or 693 yards (634 m) total
	• Color: Paul Newman
Needles	• U.S. size 8/5 mm (32" [80 cm]) circular needle
Gauge	• 16½ st and 22 rows = 4" (10 cm) in stockinette stitch, blocked
Notions	• Darning needle to weave in ends

STITCH GLOSSARY

[ ]	brackets always indicate a repeat
BO	bind off
CO	cast on
dec	decrease
inc	increase
k	knit
k2tog	knit 2 st together (dec 1)
kfb	knit into front and back of same st (inc 1)
p	purl
rep	repeat
RS	right side
ssk	slip, slip, knit 2 together (dec 1)
st	stitch/stitches
WS	wrong side

EARLY FROST SHAWL PATTERN

With U.S. size 8/5 mm (32" [80 cm]) circular needle, CO 2 st using the cable cast-on method.

ROW 1 (RS): K2.

ROW 2 (WS) AND ALL WS ROWS UNTIL OTHERWISE STATED: K.

ROW 3 (RS): K1, kfb (3 st).

ROW 5 (RS): K1, kfb, k1 (4 st).

ROW 7 (RS): K2, kfb, k1 (5 st).

ROW 9 (RS): K to 2 st before end, kfb, k1 (6 st).

ROW 11 (RS): Rep row 9 (7 st).

ROW 13 (RS): Rep row 9 (8 st).

ROW 15 (RS): K6, [kfb, k1] to end (9 st).

ROW 17 (RS): K2, ssk, k to 4 st before end, [kfb, k1] rep to end (10 st).

ROW 19 (RS): Rep row 17 (11 st).

ROW 21 (RS): K2, ssk, k to 6 st before end, [kfb, k1] rep to end (13 st).

ROW 23 (RS): Rep row 17 (14 st).

ROW 25 (RS): Rep row 21 (16 st).

ROW 27 (RS): Rep row 17 (17 st).

ROW 29 (RS): Rep row 21 (19 st).

ROW 31 (RS): Rep row 17 (20 st).

ROW 33 (RS): Rep row 21 (22 st).

ROW 35 (RS): Rep row 17 (23 st).

ROW 37 (RS): Rep row 21 (25 st).

ROW 39 (RS): Rep row 17 (26 st).

ROW 41 (RS): Rep row 21 (28 st).

ROW 43 (RS): Rep row 17 (29 st).

PATTERN SERIES

ROW 45 (RS): K2, ssk, [kfb] to end of row (53 st).

ROW 46 (WS): P.

ROW 47 (RS): K2, ssk, k to 6 st before end, [kfb, k1] to end (55 st).

ROW 48 (WS): P.

ROW 49 (RS): K2, ssk, k to 4 st before end, [kfb, k1] to end (56 st).

ROW 50 (WS): P.

ROW 51 (RS): K2, ssk, [k2tog] to last 6 st, k to end (32 st).

ROW 52 (WS): K.

ROW 53 (RS): K2, ssk, k to 6 st before end, [kfb, k1] to end (34 st).

ROW 54 (WS): K.

ROW 55 (RS): K2, ssk, k to 4 st before end, [kfb, k1] to end (35 st).

ROW 56 (WS): K.

REP rows 45–56 until you have 131 st. Please note that the stitch count for each row will grow with each additional repeat.

STOCKINETTE RUFFLE

WORK rows 45–50 once more (noting that stitch count will grow with additional repeats).

NEXT ROW, BO in knit with medium loose tension (not too loose, not too tight).

WET BLOCK flat, pinning the shawl taut to draw out the shape. Let dry.

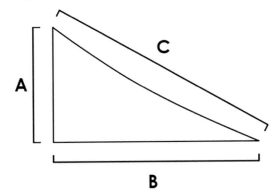

FINISHED MEASUREMENTS

A: 50" (127 cm) bind-off edge

B: 53" (135 cm) bottom edge

C: 74" (188 cm) top edge

Blizzard Funnel Wrap

I'm not naturally a winter person, unless by "winter" we're talking about staying inside by a roaring fire, knitting and drinking a hot toddy while watching the weather happen through a window. Being out in it is another story. Having recently been stranded in a blizzard in rural Michigan, I am more convinced than ever that chunky wool accessories are essential—especially in areas prone to extreme weather. The Blizzard Funnel Wrap features ridges of garter and slipped stitch sections that work beautifully together in this ultra-cozy, funnel-shape wrap. Buttons provide versatility for additional styling options.

TIMELINE

With the majority of the project being stockinette stitch with only periodic sequences of texture, this project will go quickly and can be finished in about 6 days if you work through approximately 200 yards (183 m or 1 skein) of yarn per day.

CONSTRUCTION

Knit flat from the top down, this wrap starts at the neck and grows with increases as it wraps around the shoulders. Slipped stitch garter ridges are worked in sets along the way for textural interest. Work quickly with size 9/5.5 mm needles, and you'll finish in no time!

SKILL LEVEL

Advanced Beginner

SIZE

One size fits most (see schematic for finished measurements)

MATERIALS

Yarn	• Bulky weight | Brooklyn Tweed Quarry | 100% Targhee-Columbia wool | 200 yards (183 m) per 100 g skein | 4 skeins or 800 yards (732 m) total
	• Color: Slate
Needles	• U.S. size 9/5.5 mm (32" [80 cm]) circular needle
	• U.S. size 7/4.5 mm (32" [80 cm]) circular needle for front band

MATERIALS

Gauge	• 14 st and 21 rows = 4" (10 cm) in stockinette stitch (blocked)
	• Darning needle to weave in ends
Notions	• 15 buttons (20–22 mm)
	• Needle and thread, to sew on buttons

STITCH GLOSSARY

[ ]	brackets always indicate a repeat
BO	bind off
CO	cast on
dec	decrease
inc	increase
k	knit
k2tog	knit 2 st together (dec 1)
kfb	knit into front and back of same st (inc 1)
p	purl
RS	right side
st	stitch/stitches
WS	wrong side
yo	yarn over (inc 1)

BLIZZARD FUNNEL WRAP PATTERN

With U.S. size 9/5.5 mm (32" [80 cm]) circular needle, CO 85 st using the cable cast-on method.

KNIT 8 rows.

ROW 9 (RS): K.

ROW 10 (WS): P.

ROW 11 (RS): K.

ROW 12 (WS): P.

ROW 13 (RS): K.

ROW 14 (WS): P.

ROW 15 (RS): K2, [k1, p4] to last 3 st, k3.

ROW 16 (WS): P3, [K4, p1] to last 2 st, p2.

REP rows 9–16 twice more (for a total of 3).

NEXT ROW (RS): K2, [k4, kfb] to last 8 st, k to end (15 st inc = 100 st).

NEXT ROW (WS): P.

TEXTURE PANEL

NEXT ROW (RS): K.

NEXT ROW (WS): P.

NEXT ROW (RS): K.

NEXT ROW (WS): P.

NEXT ROW (RS): K.

NEXT ROW (WS): P.

NEXT ROW (RS): K2, [k1, p4] to last 3 st, k3.

NEXT ROW (WS): P3, [K4, p1] to last 2 st, p2.

REP the Texture Panel (over 8 rows) twice more (for a total of 3).

SPACING ROWS

NEXT ROW (RS): K1, kfb, [k4, kfb] to last 3 st, k to end (20 st inc = 120 st).

NEXT ROW (WS): P.

TEXTURE PANEL

NEXT ROW (RS): K.

NEXT ROW (WS): P.

NEXT ROW (RS): K.

NEXT ROW (WS): P.

NEXT ROW (RS): K.

NEXT ROW (WS): P.

NEXT ROW (RS): K2, [k1, p4] to last 3 st, k3.

NEXT ROW (WS): P3, [K4, p1] to last 2 st, p2.

REP the Texture Panel (over 8 rows) 3 times more (for a total of 4).

NEXT ROW (RS): K2, kfb, [k3, kfb] to last 5 st, k2, kfb, k2 (30 st inc = 150 st).

NEXT ROW (WS): P.

NEXT ROW (RS): K.

NEXT ROW (WS): P.

NEXT ROW (RS): K.

NEXT ROW (WS): P.

NEXT ROW (RS): K.

NEXT ROW (WS): P.

NEXT ROW (RS): K2, [k1, p4] to last 3 st, k3.

NEXT ROW (WS): P3, [K4, p1] to last 2 st, p2.

REP the Texture Panel (over 8 rows) 3 times more (for a total of 4).

NEXT ROW (RS): K2, kfb, [k4, kfb] to last 2 st, k to end (30 st inc = 180 st).

NEXT ROW (WS): P.

NEXT ROW (RS): K.

NEXT ROW (WS): P.

NEXT ROW (RS): K.

NEXT ROW (WS): P.

NEXT ROW (RS): K.

NEXT ROW (WS): P.

NEXT ROW (RS): K2, [k1, p4] to last 3 st, k3.

NEXT ROW (WS): P3, [K4, p1] to last 2 st, p2.

REP the Texture Panel (over 8 rows) 3 times more (for a total of 4).

NEXT ROW (RS): K2, [k4, kfb] to last 3 st, k to end (35 st inc = 215 st).

NEXT ROW (WS): P.

NEXT ROW (RS): K.

NEXT ROW (WS): P.

NEXT ROW (RS): K.

NEXT ROW (WS): P.

NEXT ROW (RS): K.

NEXT ROW (WS): P.

NEXT ROW (RS): K2, [k1, p4] to last 3 st, k3.

NEXT ROW (WS): P3, [K4, p1] to last 2 st, p2.

REP the Texture Panel (over 8 rows) 6 times more (for a total of 7).

WORK 8 rows in garter st and BO with medium loose tension.

BUTTON BAND

NOTE: "Left front" and "right front" are as if you were wearing the garment. Buttonholes should be placed along your right front, and the button placement will be on the left front.

BEGINNING at lower right edge with U.S. size 7/4.5 mm (32" [80 cm]) circular needle (or needle one size smaller than used for the body of the wrap), pick up 120 st (or roughly 3 st for every 4 rows—adjust as necessary for a nice edge). Work 6 rows in garter stitch (knitting every row). Begin buttonholes on the next row as follows:

K3, [yo, k2tog, k6] to end of row, ending the last repeat with k3 instead of k6 (if you have picked up more or less than 120 stitches, you will need to adjust your button placement accordingly). Knit 2 more rows, then BO on the next row in knit.

PICK UP stitches on the left front in the same manner as on the right front. Knit 9 rows in garter st (knitting every row) and bind off on the next row (row 10) in knit.

BLOCK and weave in your ends.

BUTTONS

Sew the buttons in place on the left front of the wrap so they align with the buttonholes you have created. (Don't worry if the buttons feel quite a bit larger than the holes—they work together nicely and the smaller buttonhole size prevents the buttons from coming undone on their own.)

FINISHED MEASUREMENTS

A: 24" (60 cm) neckline

B: 59" (150 cm) measurement across bottom

C: 30" (76 cm) top to bottom

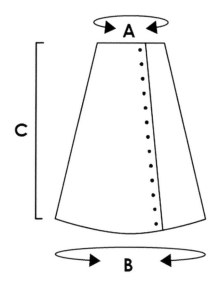

Glacier Wrap

As someone who identifies as "cold" more often than not, there is just no substitute for wool—the heartier, the better. Unbelievably dense and toasty, my Glacier Wrap takes winter weather seriously. Deep, wooly ridges and "glacier" zags of color combine for the ultimate winter wrap—it was a lifesaver on our bitter cold photoshoot day. The tightly spaced stitches create a very dense fabric for the coldest days.

TIMELINE

Knitting through about 87 yards (79 m or 1 skein) a day, the average motivated knitter can expect to finish this in 4 to 5 days. If you find that heavier yarns slow your knitting process, give yourself the full week to finish it.

CONSTRUCTION

Rectangular in shape and knit from side to side with alternating colors in an intuitive pattern repeat, Glacier is somewhere between a chubby scarf and a dense wrap.

SKILL LEVEL

Advanced Beginner

SIZE

One size fits most (see schematic for finished measurements)

MATERIALS

Yarn	• Super bulky weight | Purl Soho Super Soft Merino | 100% Merino | 87 yards (79 m) per 100 g skein | 4 skeins or 348 yards (318 m) total
	• Color A: Gray Denim 2 skeins or 174 yards (159 m)
	• Color B: Oyster Gray 2 skeins or 174 yards (159 m)
	• Yarn substitutions may create different results. Please keep this in mind.
Needles	• U.S. size 10/6 mm (32" [80 cm]) circular needle

MATERIALS

Gauge	• 21 st and 18 rows = 4" (10 cm) in pattern, blocked. (While this gauge may seem more dense than you might expect for a super bulky yarn, the stitch pattern creates a very compact fabric for extra warmth. Gauge is not essential, however, so feel free to knit yours at a looser gauge, if you prefer.)
Notions	• Darning needle to weave in ends

STITCH GLOSSARY

[ ]	brackets always indicate a repeat
BO	bind off
CO	cast on
dec	decrease
inc	increase
k	knit
k-yo-k	knit, yarn over, then knit again into the same st (2 st inc)
k2tog	knit 2 st together (dec 1)
p	purl
rep	repeat
s2kp2	slip 2 st as if to knit, k the next st on the left needle, then pass the 2 slipped st over (dec 2)
ssk	slip, slip, knit 2 together (dec 1)
yo	yarn over (inc 1)

GLACIER WRAP PATTERN

With U.S. size 10/6 mm (32" [80 cm]) circular needle and with Color A (darker grey), CO 63 st using your preferred method.

ROW 1 (WS): K.

WITH COLOR B (LIGHTER GREY)

ROW 2 (RS): K1, ssk, [k9, s2kp2] to last 12 st, k9, k2tog, k1.

ROW 3 (WS): K1, [p1, k4, k-yo-k in next st, k4] to last 2 st, p1, k1.

[WITH COLOR A: Rep rows 2 and 3

WITH COLOR B: Rep rows 2 and 3**]**

REP the series in brackets until you have worked 45 repeats and/or you are nearly out of yarn.

WORK 1 final repeat with Color A. BO in knit on the next RS row.

WEAVE IN ends and wet block flat, turning over at least once to ensure even drying.

TIP: A stick shawl pin works beautifully to keep the wrap in place.

VARIATIONS

For a less dense fabric with more drape, try using a larger needle U.S. size 13-15 (9-10 mm). If you have extra yarn and want to keep knitting, the Glacier Wrap can easily become a longer scarf.

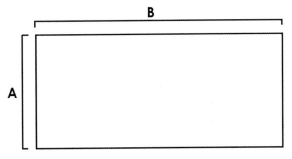

FINISHED MEASUREMENTS

A: 12" (30 cm) tall

B: 43" (109 cm) wide

Sugarplum Shawl

With a stitch pattern that is both entertaining to knit and show-stopping in its results, Sugarplum is a delightful project that will draw you in right away. It features a crescent shape with garter stitch ridges and stockinette stitch "plums" knit in cozy, worsted weight yarn. The texture is almost irresistible; I had a hard time putting it down (I bet you will, too).

TIMELINE

I knit through 1 full skein on this project during a short (3-hour) flight from Portland, Oregon, to Los Angeles, California—that's how quickly you can zip through it once you get the pattern down. Depending on your knitting speed, you can finish in just 3 days with focused knitting (about 218 yards [199 m], or 1 skein, per day). Or spread it out to 6 days by knitting through a little more than 100 yards (91 m or ½ a skein) per day, instead.

CONSTRUCTION

Sugarplum is knit from side to side, beginning with the top left corner in garter stitch and ending with the picot bind-off in the contrast color. You'll love the way the little plums form—they grow over seven rows, then "close" on the eighth row with swift decreases.

SKILL LEVEL

Intermediate

SIZE

One size fits most (see schematic for finished measurements)

MATERIALS

Yarn	
	• Worsted weight | Lolodidit Simple Worsted | 100% superwash Merino | 218 yards (199 m) per 100 g skein | 3 skeins or 654 yards (598 m) total
	• Main Color (MC): Hello Gorgeous 2 skeins or 436 yards (398 m). You will use every yard of the MC yarn.
	• Contrast Color (CC): Coal Miner's Daughter 1 partial skein or approx. 164 yards (150 m)
	• Yarn substitutions may create different results. Please keep this in mind.

MATERIALS

Needles	• U.S. size 9/5.5 mm (32" [80 cm]) circular needle
Gauge	• 17 st and 32 rows = 4" (10 cm) in garter stitch, blocked
Notions	• Darning needle to weave in ends

STITCH GLOSSARY

[ ]	brackets always indicate a repeat
bet	between
BO	bind off
CC	contrast color
CO	cast on
dec	decrease
ea	each
inc	increase
k	knit
k4tog	knit 4 st together (dec 3)
k4togtbl	knit 4 st together through back loop (dec 3)
kfb	knit into front and back of same st (inc 1)
LN	left needle
MC	main color
p	purl
rep	repeat

(continued)

ROW 3 (RS): K1, kfb (3 st).

ROW 5 (RS): K1, kfb, k1 (4 st).

ROW 7 (RS): K2, kfb, k1 (5 st).

ROW 9 (RS): K to 2 st before end, kfb, k1 (6 st).

ROW 11 (RS) : Rep row 9 (7 st).

ROW 13 (RS): Rep row 9 (8 st).

ROW 15 (RS): K6, [kfb, k1] to end (9 st).

ROW 17 (RS): K2, ssk, k to 4 st before end, [kfb, k1] to end (10 st).

ROW 19 (RS): Rep row 17 (11 st).

ROW 21 (RS): K2, ssk, k to 6 st before end, [kfb, k1] to end (13 st).

ROW 23 (RS): Rep row 17 (14 st).

ROW 25 (RS): Rep row 21 (16 st).

ROW 27 (RS): Rep row 17 (17 st).

ROW 29 (RS): Rep row 21 (19 st).

ROW 31 (RS): Rep row 17 (20 st).

ROW 33 (RS): Rep row 21 (22 st).

ROW 35 (RS): Rep row 17 (23 st).

ROW 37 (RS): Rep row 21 (25 st).

ROW 39 (RS): Rep row 17 (26 st).

ROW 41 (RS): Rep row 21 (28 st).

ROW 43 (RS): Rep row 17 (29 st).

ROW 45 (RS): Rep row 21 (31 st).

ROW 47 (RS): K2, ssk, k3, [yo, k8, yo, k1] twice, [kfb, k1] 3 times (37 st).

STITCH GLOSSARY

RN	right needle
RS	right side
ssk	slip, slip, knit 2 together (dec 1)
st	stitch/stitches
WS	wrong side
yo	yarn over (inc 1)

SUGARPLUM SHAWL PATTERN

With U.S. size 9/5.5 mm (32" [80 cm]) circular needle, and using the MC, CO 2 st using the cable cast-on method.

ROW 1 (RS): K2.

ROW 2 (WS) AND ALL WS ROWS UNTIL OTHERWISE STATED: K.

ROW 48 (WS): K11, p8, k3, p8, k7.

ROW 49 (RS): K2, ssk, k3, yo, k8, yo, k3, yo, k8, yo, k7, [kfb, k1] twice (42 st).

ROW 50 (WS): K14, p8, k5, p8, k7.

ROW 51 (RS): K2, ssk, k3, [yo, k8, yo, k5] twice, remove k3, [kfb, k1] 3 times (48 st).

ROW 52 (WS): K18, p8, k7, p8, k7.

ROW 53 (RS): K2, ssk, k3, k4togtbl, k4tog, k7, k4togtbl, k4tog, k14, [kfb, k1] twice (37 st).

ROW 54 (WS): K.

REP rows 17 and 21 (beginning with row 21) for the RS rows, knitting all WS rows, until you have 49 st and have completed a WS row.

ROW 71 (RS): K2, ssk, k3, [yo, k8, yo, k1] 4 times, k2, [kfb, k1] twice (58 st).

ROW 72 (WS): K9, p9, [k3, p8] 3 times, k to end.

ROW 73 (RS): K2, ssk, k3, [yo, k8, yo, k3] 4 times, k1, [kfb, k1] 3 times (68 st).

ROW 74 (WS): K14, p8, [k5, p8] 3 times, k7.

ROW 75 (RS): K2, ssk, k3, [yo, k8, yo, k5] 4 times, k5, [kfb, k1] twice (77 st).

ROW 76 (WS): K17, [p8, k7] to end.

ROW 77 (RS): K2, ssk, k3, [k4togtbl, k4tog, k7] 4 times, k4, [kfb, k1] 3 times (55 st).

REP rows 17 and 21 on the RS rows, knitting all WS rows, until you have 67 st and have completed a WS row.

ROW 95 (RS): K2, ssk, k3, [yo, k8, yo, k1] 6 times, k2, [kfb, k1] twice (80 st).

ROW 96 (WS): K to first yo (knit the yo, too), [p8, k3] 6 times, k to end.

ROW 97 (RS): K2, ssk, k3, [yo, k8, yo, k3] 6 times, k1, [kfb, k1] 3 times (94 st).

ROW 98 (WS): K to first yo (knit the yo, too), [p8, k5] 5 times, p8, k7.

ROW 99 (RS): K2, ssk, k3, [yo, k8, yo, k5] 6 times, k5, [kfb, k1] twice (107 st).

ROW 100 (WS): K to the first yo (knit the yo, too), [p8, k7] to end.

ROW 101 (RS): K2, ssk, k3, [k4togtbl, k4tog, k7] 6 times, k4, [kfb, k1] 3 times (73 st).

REP rows 17 and 21 on the RS rows, knitting all WS rows, until you have 85 st and have completed a WS row.

ROW 119 (RS): K2, ssk, k3, [yo, k8, yo, k1] 8 times, k2, [kfb, k1] twice (102 st).

ROW 120 (WS): K to first yo (knit the yo, too), [p8, k3] 8 times, k to end.

ROW 121 (RS): K2, ssk, k3, [yo, k8, yo, k3] 8 times, k1, [kfb, k1] 3 times (120 st).

ROW 147 (RS): K2, ssk, k3, [yo, k8, yo, k5] 10 times, k5, [kfb, k1] twice (167 st).

ROW 148 (WS): K to first yo (k the yo, too), [p8, k7] to end.

ROW 149 (RS): K2, ssk, k3, [k4togtbl, k4tog, k7] 10 times, k4, [kfb, k1] 3 times (109 st).

REP rows 17 and 21 on the RS rows, knitting all WS rows, until you have 121 st and have completed a WS row.

ROW 167 (RS): K2, ssk, k3, [yo, k8, yo, k1] 12 times, k1, [kfb, k1] twice (146 st).

ROW 168 (WS): K to first yo (knit the yo, too), [p8, k3] 12 times, k to end.

ROW 169 (RS): K2, ssk, k3, [yo, k8, yo, k3] 12 times, k1, [kfb, k1] 3 times (172 st).

ROW 170 (WS): K to first yo (k the yo, too), [p8, k5] 12 times, k2.

ROW 171 (RS): K2, ssk, k3, [yo, k8, yo, k5] 12 times, k5, [kfb, k1] twice (197 st).

ROW 172 (WS): K to first yo (k the yo, too), [p8, k7] to end.

ROW 173 (RS): K2, ssk, k3, [k4togtbl, k4tog, k7] 12 times, k4, [kfb, k1] 3 times (127 st).

REP rows 17 and 21 on the RS rows, knitting all WS rows, until you have 139 st and have completed a WS row.

ROW 191 (RS): K2, ssk, k3, [yo, k8, yo, k1] 14 times, k2, [kfb, k1] twice (168 st).

ROW 192 (WS): K to first yo (knit the yo, too), [p8, k3] 14 times, k to end.

ROW 193 (RS): K2, ssk, k3, [yo, k8, yo, k3] 14 times, k2, [kfb, k1] 3 times (198 st).

ROW 194 (WS): K to first yo (k the yo, too), [p8, k5] 14 times, k2.

ROW 195 (RS): K2, ssk, k3, [yo, k8, yo, k5] 14 times, k5, [kfb, k1] twice (227 st).

ROW 196 (WS): K to first yo (k the yo, too), [p8, k7] to end.

ROW 122 (WS): K to first yo (k the yo, too), [p8, k5] 8 times, k7.

ROW 123 (RS): K2, ssk, k3, [yo, k8, yo, k5] 8 times, k5, [kfb, k1] twice (137 st).

ROW 124 (WS): K to first yo (k the yo, too), [p8, k7] to end.

ROW 125 (RS): K2, ssk, k3, [k4togtbl, k4tog, k7] 8 times, k4, [kfb, k1] 3 times (91 st).

REP rows 17 and 21 on the RS rows, knitting all WS rows, until you have 103 st and have completed a WS row.

ROW 143 (RS): K2, ssk, k3, [yo, k8, yo, k1] 10 times, k2, [kfb, k1] twice (124 st).

ROW 144 (WS): K to first yo (knit the yo, too), [p8, k3] 10 times, k to end.

ROW 145 (RS): K2, ssk, k3, [yo, k8, yo, k3] 10 times, k1, [kfb, k1] 3 times (146 st).

ROW 146 (WS): K to first yo (k the yo, too), [p8, k5] 10 times, k2.

ROW 197 (RS): K2, ssk, k3, [k4togtbl, k4tog, k7] 14 times, k4, [kfb, k1] 3 times (145 st).

REP rows 17 and 21 on the RS rows, knitting all WS rows, until you have 157 st and have completed a WS row.

ROW 215 (RS): K2, ssk, k3, [yo, k8, yo, k1] 16 times, k2, [kfb, k1] twice (190 st).

ROW 216 (WS): K to first yo (knit the yo, too), [p8, k3] 16 times, k to end.

ROW 217 (RS): K2, ssk, k3, [yo, k8, yo, k3] 16 times, k1, [kfb, k1] 3 times (224 st).

ROW 218 (WS): K to first yo (k the yo, too), [p8, k5] 16 times, k2.

ROW 219 (RS): K2, ssk, k3, [yo, k8, yo, k5] 16 times, k5, [kfb, k1] twice (257 st).

ROW 220 (WS): K to first yo (k the yo, too), [p8, k7] to end.

CUT MC and join CC to continue. CC will be used for remainder of work.

ROW 221 (RS): K2, ssk, k3, [k4togtbl, k4tog, k7] 16 times, k4, [kfb, k1] 3 times (163 st).

ROW 222 (WS): K.

ROW 223 (RS): K2, ssk, k to 4 st before end, [kfb, k1] to end (1 st inc).

ROW 224 (WS): K.

ROW 225 (RS): K2, ssk, k to 6 st before end, [kfb, k1] rep to end (2 st inc).

ROW 226 (WS): K.

REP rows 223–226 twice more.

PICOT BIND-OFF

At the start of the row, [CO 2 st using any method, BO 4 st (including the 2 st you cast on), slide the last st from the RN back to the LN]. Rep bet brackets until you've reached the end of the row, binding off any last st that remain after the last picot is made.

WEAVE IN all ends and wet block, pinning flat and stretching the shawl out flat and taut, pinning the edges straight until dry.

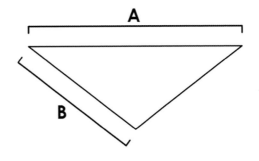

FINISHED MEASUREMENTS

A: 59" (150 cm) from wingtip to wingtip

B: 40" (102 cm) from wingtip to center point

Deep, dark winter, here we come! Dense ridges and tidy cables partner for an ultra-cozy, incredibly warm shawl that will take the edge off on even the coldest of January days. Small in size, the January Morning Shawl can tuck into your coat without excess bulk (but you can keep adding to the size if you want a more generous shawl).

TIMELINE

Knit in heavyweight yarn with minimal construction details, you can easily knit this shawl during a long weekend. Plan on knitting through about 110 yards (101 m or about ⅔ of a skein) per day to finish in 3 days. The simple repetition means easier knitting on the go or while visiting with friends.

CONSTRUCTION

Knit diagonally from the side corner to the far edge with garter stitch ridges and a band of cables, January Morning is a quick knit with consistent texture that requires little focus.

SKILL LEVEL

Intermediate

SIZE

One size fits most (see schematic for finished measurements)

MATERIALS

Yarn	• Aran weight | Purl Soho Worsted Twist | 100% Merino | 164 yards (150 m) per 100 g skein | 2 skeins or 328 yards (300 m) total
	• Color: Oatmeal Grey
	• Yarn substitutions may create different results. Please keep this in mind.
Needles	• U.S. size 8/5 mm (32" [80 cm]) circular needle
Gauge	• 13 st and 29 rows = 4" (10 cm) in garter stitch, blocked
	• Cable needle
Notions	• Stitch markers, including a locking marker
	• Darning needle to weave in ends

STITCH GLOSSARY

[ ]	brackets always indicate a repeat
BO	bind off
CO	cast on
c6f	cable 6 front (place 3 st on cable needle and hold to front, knit the next 3 st on the left needle, then knit the 3 st from the cable needle). Note: The cable is a 6-row repeat.
k	knit
kfb	knit into front and back of same st (inc 1)
m	marker
p	purl
pm	place marker
rep	repeat
RS	right side
sm	slip marker
st	stitch or stitches
WS	wrong side

JANUARY MORNING SHAWL PATTERN

With U.S. size 8/5 mm (32" [80 cm]) circular needle, CO 2 st using the cable cast-on method.

ROW 1 (RS): Kfb, k1.

ROW 2 (WS): K.

ROW 3 (RS): K1, kfb, k1 (attach a locking marker anywhere on this side to help keep track of the right side).

ROW 4 (WS): K.

ROW 5 (RS): K1, kfb, k to end.

ROW 6 (WS): K.

REP rows 5 and 6 until you have 13 st.

NEXT ROW (RS): K1, kfb, k1, pm, k6, pm, k to end (14 st).

NEXT ROW (WS): K to m, sm, p6, sm, k to end.

NEXT ROW (RS): K1, kfb, k to m, sm, c6f, sm, k to end (15 st).

NEXT ROW (WS): K to m, sm, p6, sm, k to end.

[**NEXT ROW (RS):** K1, kfb, k to m, sm, k6, sm, k to end (16 st).

NEXT ROW (WS): K to m, sm, p6, sm, k to end.]

REP these 2 rows between brackets once more (17 st).

REPEAT SECTION

ROW 1 (RS): K1, kfb, k to m, sm, c6f, sm, k to end (1 st inc).

ROW 2 (WS): K to m, sm, p6, sm, k to end.

ROW 3 (RS): K1, kfb, k to m, sm, k6, sm, k to end (1 st inc).

ROW 4 (WS): K to m, sm, p6, sm, k to end.

ROW 5 (RS): K1, kfb, k to m, sm, k6, sm, k to end (1 st inc).

ROW 6 (WS): K to m, sm, p6, sm, k to end.

CONTINUE working the Repeat Section (repeating rows 1 through 6) until you have 106 st.

FINAL EDGE

NEXT ROW (RS): K1, kfb, k to end.

NEXT ROW (WS): K across.

REP the Final Edge rows 2 more times (for a total of 3). Remove markers as you go.

BO on the next row (on the RS) in knit with medium loose tension.

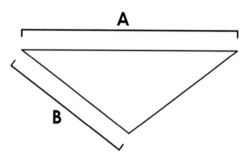

FINISHED MEASUREMENTS

A: 35" (89 cm)

B: 48" (122 cm)

Fallen Petals Shawl

I love the color of the roses outside my office window and am always disappointed to see them lose their petals at the end of the season. Then again, this natural process makes way for new buds in the spring. The deep, rich color of this shawl is adorned with rows of simple lace "buds" throughout. The moderately loose gauge expands and drapes beautifully with blocking, making it large enough to wrap double for extra warmth.

TIMELINE

This is a moderately simple project with minimal focus required. A motivated knitter can work through this project in about 7 days by knitting approximately ½ a skein (or 109 yards [100 m]) each day.

CONSTRUCTION

Knit from the smallest point to the far edge, Fallen Petals is worked with staggered increases along one edge. The result is a shape somewhere between an elongated triangle and a boomerang. The lace insert will inspire light focus, without slowing your progress.

SKILL LEVEL

Advanced Beginner

SIZE

One size fits most (see schematic for finished measurements)

MATERIALS

Yarn	• Worsted weight | Lolodidit Simple Worsted | 100% superwash Merino | 218 yards (199 m) per 100 g skein | 4 skeins or 872 yards (797 m) total • Color: Red, Red Wine
Needles	• U.S. size 8/5 mm (32" [80 cm]) circular needle
Gauge	• 16 st and 22 rows = 4" (10 cm) in stockinette stitch, blocked
Notions	• Stitch markers, including a locking marker • Darning needle to weave in ends

STITCH GLOSSARY

[ ]	brackets always indicate a repeat
bet	between
BO	bind off
CO	cast on
dec	decrease
inc	increase
k	knit
k2tog	knit 2 st together (dec 1)
kfb	knit into front and back of same st (inc 1)
m	marker
p	purl
pm	place marker
rep	repeat
RS	right side
sl1-k1-psso	slip 1 st without working it, k the next st, then slip the first st (the one you slipped) over the k st (dec 1)
sl1-k2tog-psso	slip 1 st without working it, k the next 2 st together, then slip the first st (the one you slipped) over the st you knit together (dec 2)
sm	slip marker
st	stitch/stitches
WS	wrong side
yo	yarn over (inc 1)

FALLEN PETALS SHAWL PATTERN

With U.S. size 8/5 mm (32" [80 cm]) circular needle, and using your preferred cast-on method, CO 2 st.

ROW 1 (RS): Kfb, k1 (3 st).

ROW 2 (WS): P.

ROW 3 (RS): K1, kfb, k1 (attach a locking marker anywhere on this side to help keep track of the right side) (4 st).

ROW 4 (WS): P.

ROW 5 (RS): K1, kfb, k to end (5 st).

ROW 6 (WS): K3, p to end.

REP rows 5 and 6 until you have 22 st.

NEXT ROW (RS): K1, kfb, pm, k1, yo, k3, sl1-k1-psso, p5, k2tog, k3, yo, k1, pm, k3 (23 st).

NEXT ROW (WS): K3, sm, p6, k5, p6, sm, p to end.

NEXT ROW (RS): K1, kfb, k to m, sm, k2, yo, k3, sl1-k1-psso, p3, k2tog, k3, yo, k2, sm, k3 (24 st).

NEXT ROW (WS): K3, sm, p7, k3, p7, sm, p to end.

NEXT ROW (RS): K1, kfb, k to m, sm, k3, yo, k3, sl1-k1-psso, p1, k2tog, k3, yo, k3, sm, k3 (25 st).

NEXT ROW (WS): K3, sm, p8, k1, p8, sm, p to end.

NEXT ROW (RS): K1, kfb, k to m, sm, k4, yo, k3, sl1-k2tog-psso, k3, yo, k4, sm, k3 (26 st).

NEXT ROW (WS): K3, p to end, slipping markers as you go.

NEXT ROW (RS): K1, kfb, k to end (1 st inc)—remove first marker on this row (leave last marker) (27 st).

NEXT ROW (WS): K3, sm, p to end.

REP these last 2 rows until you have 39 st.

NEXT ROW (RS): K1, kfb, pm, [k1, yo, k3, sl1-k1-psso, p5, k2tog, k3, yo, k1] twice, sm, k3 (40 st).

NEXT ROW (WS): K3, sm, [p6, k5, p6] twice, sm, p to end.

NEXT ROW (RS): K1, kfb, k to m, sm, [k2, yo, k3, sl1-k1-psso, p3, k2tog, k3, yo, k2] twice, sm, k3 (41 st).

NEXT ROW (WS): K3, sm, [p7, k3, p7] twice, sm, p to end.

NEXT ROW (RS): K1, kfb, k to m, sm, [k3, yo, k3, sl1-k1-psso, p1, k2tog, k3, yo, k3] twice, sm, k3 (42 st).

NEXT ROW (WS): K3, sm, [p8, k1, p8] twice, sm, p to end.

NEXT ROW (RS): K1, kfb, k to m, sm, [k4, yo, k3, sl1-k2tog-psso, k3, yo, k4] twice, sm, k3 (43 st).

NEXT ROW (WS): K3, p to end, slipping markers as you go.

NEXT ROW (RS): K1, kfb, k to end (1 st inc)—remove first marker on this row (leave last marker) (44 st).

NEXT ROW (WS): K3, sm, p to end.

REP these last 2 rows until you have 56 st.

NEXT ROW (RS): K1, kfb, pm, [k1, yo, k3, sl1-k1-psso, p5, k2tog, k3, yo, k1] 3 times, sm, k3 (57 st).

NEXT ROW (WS): K3, sm, [p6, k5, p6] 3 times, sm, p to end.

NEXT ROW (RS): K1, kfb, k to m, sm, [k2, yo, k3, sl1-k1-psso, p3, k2tog, k3, yo, k2] 3 times, sm, k3 (58 st).

NEXT ROW (WS): K3, sm, [p7, k3, p7] 3 times, sm, p to end.

NEXT ROW (RS): K1, kfb, k to m, sm, [k3, yo, k3, sl1-k1-psso, p1, k2tog, k3, yo, k3] 3 times, sm, k3 (59 st).

NEXT ROW (WS): K3, sm, [p8, k1, p8] 3 times, sm, p to end.

NEXT ROW (RS): K1, kfb, k to m, sm, [k4, yo, k3, sl1-k2tog-psso, k3, yo, k4] 3 times, sm, k3 (60 st).

NEXT ROW (WS): K3, p to end, slipping markers as you go.

NEXT ROW (RS): K1, kfb, k to end (1 st inc)—remove first marker on this row (leave last marker).

NEXT ROW (WS): K3, sm, p to end.

REP these last 2 rows until you have 73 st.

NEXT ROW (RS): K1, kfb, pm, [k1, yo, k3, sl1-k1-psso, p5, k2tog, k3, yo, k1] 4 times, sm, k3 (74 st).

NEXT ROW (WS): K3, sm, [p6, k5, p6] 4 times, sm, p to end.

NEXT ROW (RS): K1, kfb, k to m, sm, [k2, yo, k3, sl1-k1-psso, p3, k2tog, k3, yo, k2] 4 times, sm, k3 (75 st).

NEXT ROW (WS): K3, sm, [p7, k3, p7] 4 times, sm, p to end.

NEXT ROW (RS): K1, kfb, k to m, sm, [k3, yo, k3, sl1-k1-psso, p1, k2tog, k3, yo, k3] 4 times, sm, k3 (76 st).

NEXT ROW (WS): K3, sm, [p8, k1, p8] 4 times, sm, p to end.

NEXT ROW (RS): K1, kfb, k to m, sm, [k4, yo, k3, sl1-k2tog-psso, k3, yo, k4] 4 times, sm, k3 (77 st).

NEXT ROW (WS): K3, p to end, slipping markers as you go.

NEXT ROW (RS): K1, kfb, k to end (1 st inc)—remove first marker on this row (leave last marker).

NEXT ROW (WS): K3, sm, p to end.

REP these last 2 rows until you have 90 st.

NEXT ROW (RS): K1, kfb, pm, [k1, yo, k3, sl1-k1-psso, p5, k2tog, k3, yo, k1] 5 times, sm, k3 (91 st).

NEXT ROW (WS): K3, sm, [p6, k5, p6] 5 times, sm, p to end.

NEXT ROW (RS): K1, kfb, k to m, sm, [k2, yo, k3, sl1-k1-psso, p3, k2tog, k3, yo, k2] 5 times, sm, k3 (92 st).

NEXT ROW (WS): K3, sm, [p7, k3, p7] 5 times, sm, p to end.

NEXT ROW (RS): K1, kfb, k to m, sm, [k3, yo, k3, sl1-k1-psso, p1, k2tog, k3, yo, k3] 5 times, sm, k3 (93 st).

NEXT ROW (WS): K3, sm, [p8, k1, p8] 5 times, sm, p to end.

NEXT ROW (RS): K1, kfb, k to m, sm, [k4, yo, k3, sl1-k2tog-psso, k3, yo, k4] 5 times, sm, k3 (94 st).

NEXT ROW (WS): K3, p to end, slipping markers as you go.

NEXT ROW (RS): K1, kfb, k to end (1 st inc)—remove first marker on this row (leave last marker).

NEXT ROW (WS): K3, sm, p to end.

REP these last 2 rows until you have 107 st.

NEXT ROW (RS): K1, kfb, pm, [k1, yo, k3, sl1-k1-psso, p5, k2tog, k3, yo, k1] 6 times, sm, k3 (108 st).

NEXT ROW (WS): K3, sm, [p6, k5, p6] 6 times, sm, p to end.

NEXT ROW (RS): K1, kfb, k to m, sm, [k2, yo, k3, sl1-k1-psso, p3, k2tog, k3, yo, k2] 6 times, sm, k3 (109 st).

NEXT ROW (WS): K3, sm, [p7, k3, p7] 6 times, sm, p to end.

NEXT ROW (RS): K1, kfb, k to m, sm, [k3, yo, k3, sl1-k1-psso, p1, k2tog, k3, yo, k3] 6 times, sm, k3 (110 st).

NEXT ROW (WS): K3, sm, [p8, k1, p8] 6 times, sm, p to end.

NEXT ROW (RS): K1, kfb, k to m, sm, [k4, yo, k3, sl1-k2tog-psso, k3, yo, k4] 6 times, sm, k3 (111 st).

NEXT ROW (WS): K3, p to end, slipping markers as you go.

NEXT ROW (RS): K1, kfb, k to end (1 st inc)—remove first marker on this row (leave last marker).

NEXT ROW (WS): K3, sm, p to end.

REP these last 2 rows until you have 124 st.

NEXT ROW (RS): K1, kfb, pm, [k1, yo, k3, sl1-k1-psso, p5, k2tog, k3, yo, k1] 7 times, sm, k3 (125 st).

NEXT ROW (WS): K3, sm, [p6, k5, p6] 7 times, sm, p to end.

NEXT ROW (RS): K1, kfb, k to m, sm, [k2, yo, k3, sl1-k1-psso, p3, k2tog, k3, yo, k2] 7 times, sm, k3 (126 st).

NEXT ROW (WS): K3, sm, [p7, k3, p7] 7 times, sm, p to end.

NEXT ROW (RS): K1, kfb, k to m, sm, [k3, yo, k3, sl1-k1-psso, p1, k2tog, k3, yo, k3] 7 times, sm, k3 (127 st).

NEXT ROW (WS): K3, sm, [p8, k1, p8] 7 times, sm, p to end.

NEXT ROW (RS): K1, kfb, k to m, sm, [k4, yo, k3, sl1-k2tog-psso, k3, yo, k4] 7 times, sm, k3 (128 st).

NEXT ROW (WS): K3, p to end, slipping markers as you go.

NEXT ROW (RS): K1, kfb, k to end (1 st inc)—remove first marker on this row (leave last marker).

NEXT ROW (WS): K3, sm, p to end.

REP these last 2 rows until you have 141 st.

NEXT ROW (RS): K1, kfb, pm, [k1, yo, k3, sl1-k1-psso, p5, k2tog, k3, yo, k1] 8 times, sm, k3 (142 st).

NEXT ROW (WS): K3, sm, [p6, k5, p6] 8 times, sm, p to end.

NEXT ROW (RS): K1, kfb, k to m, sm, [k2, yo, k3, sl1-k1-psso, p3, k2tog, k3, yo, k2] 8 times, sm, k3 (143 st).

NEXT ROW (WS): K3, sm, [p7, k3, p7] 8 times, sm, p to end.

NEXT ROW (RS): K1, kfb, k to m, sm, [k3, yo, k3, sl1-k1-psso, p1, k2tog, k3, yo, k3] 8 times, sm, k3 (144 st).

NEXT ROW (WS): K3, sm, [p8, k1, p8] 8 times, sm, p to end.

NEXT ROW (RS): K1, kfb, k to m, sm, [k4, yo, k3, sl1-k2tog-psso, k3, yo, k4] 8 times, sm, k3 (145 st).

NEXT ROW (WS): K3, p to end, slipping markers as you go.

NEXT ROW (RS): K1, kfb, k to end (1 st inc)—remove first marker on this row (leave last marker).

NEXT ROW (WS): K3, sm, p to end.

REP these last 2 rows until you have 158 st.

NEXT ROW (RS): K1, kfb, pm, [k1, yo, k3, sl1-k1-psso, p5, k2tog, k3, yo, k1] 9 times, sm, k3 (159 st).

NEXT ROW (WS): K3, sm, [p6, k5, p6] 9 times, sm, p to end.

NEXT ROW (RS): K1, kfb, k to m, sm, [k2, yo, k3, sl1-k1-psso, p3, k2tog, k3, yo, k2] 9 times, sm, k3 (160 st).

NEXT ROW (WS): K3, sm, [p7, k3, p7] 9 times, sm, p to end.

NEXT ROW (RS): K1, kfb, k to m, sm, [k3, yo, k3, sl1-k1-psso, p1, k2tog, k3, yo, k3] 9 times, sm, k3 (161 st).

NEXT ROW (WS): K3, sm, [p8, k1, p8] 9 times, sm, p to end.

NEXT ROW (RS): K1, kfb, k to m, sm, [k4, yo, k3, sl1-k2tog-psso, k3, yo, k4] 9 times, sm, k3 (162 st).

NEXT ROW (WS): K3, p to end, slipping markers as you go.

NEXT ROW (RS): K1, kfb, k to end (1 st inc)—remove first marker on this row (leave last marker).

NEXT ROW (WS): K3, sm, p to end.

REP these last 2 rows until you have 175 st.

NEXT ROW (RS): K1, kfb, pm, [k1, yo, k3, sl1-k1-psso, p5, k2tog, k3, yo, k1] 10 times, sm, k3 (176 st).

NEXT ROW (WS): K3, sm, [p6, k5, p6] 10 times, sm, p to end.

NEXT ROW (RS): K1, kfb, k to m, sm, [k2, yo, k3, sl1-k1-psso, p3, k2tog, k3, yo, k2] 10 times, sm, k3 (177 st).

NEXT ROW (WS): K3, sm, [p7, k3, p7] 10 times, sm, p to end.

NEXT ROW (RS): K1, kfb, k to m, sm, [k3, yo, k3, sl1-k1-psso, p1, k2tog, k3, yo, k3] 10 times, sm, k3 (178 st).

NEXT ROW (WS): K3, sm, [p8, k1, p8] 10 times, sm, p to end.

NEXT ROW (RS): K1, kfb, k to m, sm, [k4, yo, k3, sl1-k2tog-psso, k3, yo, k4] 10 times, sm, k3 (179 st).

NEXT ROW (WS): K3, p to end—remove markers as you work this row.

NEXT ROW (RS): K1, kfb, k to end.

NEXT ROW (WS): BO in k with medium loose tension.

WEAVE IN ends and wet block, drawing the shawl taut on the blocking mat and pinning in place until dry.

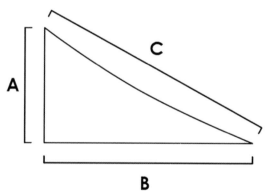

FINISHED MEASUREMENTS

A: 43" (109 cm) bind-off edge

B: 62" (157 cm) bottom edge

C: 74" (188 cm) top edge

Hibernate Wrap

A dainty, vintage lace stitch (which reminds me of a prayer shawl) brings an air of femininity to this unconventional buttoned wrap. Hibernate can be worn over the shoulders, partially buttoned, or even as a wide, loose cowl.

TIMELINE

With all-over texture and buttonholes, this project can take a bit more focus. Working at a pace of approximately 115 yards (105 m) (or about ⅔ of a skein per day), you can finish in about 5 days, with time left for blocking and buttons.

CONSTRUCTION

Hibernate begins with a ribbed band, followed by an increase row just before you begin the lace. It's knit side to side and finished with a row of decreases, then ribbing and buttonholes. By buttoning the wrap in different formations, you can increase the versatility of this unique piece.

TIP

If you have extra yarn and would like to have more room around the shoulders, simply continue working the lace section until you have an additional 6 to 8 inches (15 to 20 cm) of length. Then work the remainder of the pattern as written.

SKILL LEVEL

Intermediate

SIZE

One size fits most (see schematic for finished measurements)

MATERIALS

Yarn	• Aran weight | HiKoo Simplinatural | 40% baby alpaca, 40% fine Merino wool, 20% mulberry silk | 183 yards (167 m) per 100 g skein | 4 skeins or 732 yards (669 m) total
	• Color: Natural
	• Yarn substitutions may create different results. Please keep this in mind.

MATERIALS

Needles	• U.S. size 8/5 mm (32" [80 cm]) circular needle
Gauge	• 21½ st and 26 rows = 4" (10 cm) in lace pattern, blocked
Notions	• Darning needle to weave in ends
	• 5 buttons (15 mm)
	• Needle and thread to sew on buttons

STITCH GLOSSARY

[ ]	brackets always indicate a repeat
BO	bind off
CO	cast on
dec	decrease
inc	increase
k	knit
k2tog	knit 2 st together (dec 1)
k3tog	knit 3 st together (dec 2)
k3togtbl	knit 3 st together through the back loop (dec 2)
kfb	knit into front and back of same st (inc 1)
p	purl
rep	repeat
RS	right side
st	stitch/stitches
WS	wrong side
yo	yarn over (inc 1)

HIBERNATE WRAP PATTERN

With U.S. size 8/5 mm (32" [80 cm]) circular needle, CO 54 st using the cable cast-on method.

RIBBED EDGING

ROW 1 (RS): K2, [p2, k2] to end.

ROW 2 (WS): P2, [k2, p2] to end.

REP these 2 edging rows 4 more times (for a total of 5 repeats).

INC ROW

ROW 1 (RS): K3, [kfb] to last 3 st, k3 (102 st).

ROW 2 (WS): P across.

LACE PATTERN

ROW 1 (RS): K3, [p2, k3tog, yo, k1, yo, k1, yo, k1, yo, k3togtbl, p1] rep to last 3 st, k3.

ROW 2 (WS): P3, [k1, p9, k2] rep to last 3 st, p3.

ROW 3 (RS): K3, [k1, yo, k1, yo, k3tog, p3, k3togtbl, yo, k1, yo] rep to last 3 st, k3.

ROW 4 (WS): P3, [p4, k3, p5] rep to last 3 st, p3.

REP rows 1–4 of Lace Pattern until the wrap measures 40" (102 cm).

DEC ROW

ROW 1 (RS): K3, [k2tog] rep to last 3 st, k3 (54 st).

ROW 2 (WS): P across.

RIBBED EDGE W/BUTTONHOLES

ROW 1 (RS): K2, [p2, k2] to end.

ROW 2 (WS): P2, [k2, p2] to end.

REP these 2 edging rows 2 more times (for a total of 3).

NEXT ROW (RS): K2, p2 [BO 2, p2, k2, p2, k2, p2] rep 3 times, BO 2, p2, k2, p2, BO 2, p2, k2.

NEXT ROW (WS): P2, k2, CO 2, k2, p2, k2, CO 2, [k2, p2, k2, p2, k2, CO 2] rep 3 times, k2, p2.

NEXT ROW (RS): K2, [p2, k2] to end.

NEXT ROW (WS): P2, [k2, p2] to end.

NEXT ROW (RS): BO in pattern.

WET BLOCK flat, pinning in place until dry.

ATTACH the buttons with a needle and thread to the ribbing on the opposite end of the buttonholes.

STITCH the buttons in place on the right side to correspond with the buttonholes.

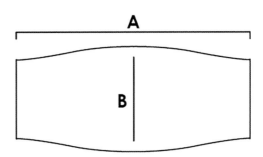

FINISHED MEASUREMENTS

A: 45" (114 cm) wide

B: 19" (48 cm) tall

Spring & Summer

My knitting doesn't slow down in the warm months. I might favor lightweight projects when the sun is out in all its glory, but I'm no stranger to a lapful of heavy wool in the middle of July (just ask my husband and knitting friends—it's a bit comical sometimes). But just because I'm one for ridiculously wooly projects on sweltering days doesn't mean that's the only option. Patterns with elongated stitches (such as Puddlejumper, page 107) or with a loose gauge (such as Thunderstorm, page 113) give you just a bit of warmth with room to breathe.

If you're not one for knitting in the warm months—or even if you are—I'm convinced that layers are just as necessary in the spring as they are in fall and winter. Spring is the moodiest season, I think, and I have more often found myself shivering at an event that was meant to be held on a warm day in the spring than any other time of the year.

The knits on the following pages are for knitting *and* wearing in the warmer months. They're for days with misleading sunshine, surprise rainstorms, windy gusts and all the other unexpected gifts of the season. You'll find lightweight shawls for cool evenings that range from casual to elegant, so that even if you find yourself at an unexpectedly cool June wedding, you'll have exactly the right thing to wear (Spring Equinox on page 89 would be lovely at a wedding, don't you think?).

Spring Equinox Wrap

There's something to be said for an elegant wrap, and while I envision myself wearing it with a cocktail dress, let's be honest—I'm more likely to wear it with a pair of jeans and Swedish clogs. Spring Equinox is a lightweight rectangle wrap with feminine details, knit in a beautiful blend of fiber that lends sheen and drape. The result is so incredibly lovely and wearable; it will become a quick favorite.

TIMELINE

The most time-consuming part of this project is that the lace pattern is worked on both the right side and the wrong side, so you'll need to give yourself the full 7 days to complete the project, with several hours available to knit each day. By working with yarn held doubled, you'll be knitting through twice the yardage at once, so to calculate your time, estimate knitting approximately 80 yards' (73 m) worth of stitches per day (but with two strands held at once, that would be 160 yards [146 m] or 1/3 of two skeins total yarn used each day). It's one of the most ambitious projects in the book, but the end result is worth the effort.

CONSTRUCTION

Spring Equinox is knit from side to side using two strands of yarn (held double) with a simple lace repeat that is worked on both the right side and the wrong side. If you'd prefer a lighter weight wrap, you can work the design with a single strand of yarn. As written, the wrap will feel a bit heavy while you're knitting it, but it will relax and expand into a lovely mid-weight accessory when blocked.

SKILL LEVEL

Intermediate

SIZE

One size fits most (see schematic for finished measurements)

MATERIALS

Yarn	• Sport weight | HiKoo Rylie | 50% alpaca, 25% mulberry silk, 25% linen | 274 yards (251 m) per 100 g skein | 4 skeins or 1,096 yards (1,002 m) total. Yarn is held double throughout
	• Color: Sandbar
	• Note: The recommended yarn will relax and drape beautifully with blocking, thanks to the natural qualities of alpaca, silk and linen. If you opt to substitute with a different kind of fiber blend (especially one that is less likely to drape), you may want to consider using a single strand of yarn.
Needles	• U.S. size 8/5 mm (32–40" [80–102 cm]) circular needle
Gauge	• 18 st and 22 rows = 4" (10 cm) in pattern stitch, blocked
Notions	• Darning needle to weave in ends

STITCH GLOSSARY

[ ]	brackets always indicate a repeat
BO	bind off
CO	cast on
dec	decrease
inc	increase
k	knit
k2tog	knit 2 st together (dec 1)
p	purl

(continued)

STITCH GLOSSARY

p2tog	purl 2 st together (dec 1)
rep	repeat
RS	right side
st	stitch/stitches
WS	wrong side
yo	yarn over (inc 1)

SPRING EQUINOX WRAP PATTERN

With U.S. size 8/5 mm (32–40" [80–102 cm]) circular needle, and holding two strands of yarn together (working them as one) CO 84 st using the cable cast-on method.

TIP: It will be easier to work with two strands if you wind your yarn into cakes and pull from the center on each.

SET-UP ROW (RS): K1, p1, k to last 2 st, p1, k1.

SET-UP ROW (WS): P1, k1, p to last 2 st, k1, p1.

NOTE: The lace section begins below. If you prefer to work from a chart, you may refer to the chart on the next page for the lace portion worked between brackets. The chart does not reflect the two edge stitches on either side of the repeat.

ROW 1 (RS): K1, p1, [k4, k2tog, k1, yo, k3] to last 2 st, p1, k1.

ROW 2 (WS): P1, k1, [p3, yo, p2, p2tog, p3] to last 2 st, k1, p1.

ROW 3 (RS): K1, p1, [k2, k2tog, k3, yo, k3] to last 2 st, p1, k1.

ROW 4 (WS): P1, k1, [p3, yo, p4, p2tog, p1] to last 2 st, k1, p1.

ROW 5 (RS): K1, p1, [k2tog, k5, yo, k3] to last 2 st, p1, k1.

ROW 6 (WS): P1, k1, [p4, p2tog, p1, yo, p3] to last 2 st, k1, p1.

ROW 7 (RS): K1, p1, [k3, yo, k2, k2tog, k3] to last 2 st, p1, k1.

ROW 8 (WS): P1, k1, [p2, p2tog, p3, yo, p3] to last 2 st, k1, p1.

ROW 9 (RS): K1, p1, [k3, yo, k4, k2tog, k1] to last 2 st, p1, k1.

ROW 10 (WS): P1, k1, [p2tog, p5, yo, p3] to last 2 st, k1, p1.

REP rows 1–10 until you've used nearly all your yarn, finishing your repeat with row 10. Work last 2 rows as follows:

END ROW 1 (RS): K1, p1, k to last 2 st, p1, k1.

END ROW 2 (WS): P1, k1, p to last 2 st, k1, p1.

BO on the next row in knit with medium tension.

WET BLOCK and pin flat, drawing the edges taut, on your blocking mat until dry.

LACE CHART

10	9	8	7	6	5	4	3	2	1	
⊘̇						O				10
	⁄					O				9
		⊘̇				O				8
			⁄			O				7
				⊘̇		O				6
				O				⁄		5
				O				⊘̇		4
				O			⁄			3
				O		⊘̇				2
				O	⁄					1

KEY

☐	k	Knit (RS) Knit (WS) Purl
⁄	k2tog	Knit 2 Together (RS) Knit 2 stitches together
⊘̇	p2tog	Purl 2 Together (WS) Purl 2 stitches together
O	yo	Yarn Over (RS) Yarn over (WS) Yarn over

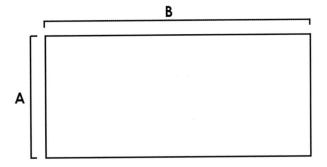

FINISHED MEASUREMENTS

A: 19" (48 cm) tall

B: 59" (150 cm) wide—length may vary based on your yardage

Walkabout Shawlette

I always want a little something with me when I go for a walk—even on sunny spring days (you never know when the weather will change its mind). This scalloped two-tone design creates a light, lovely shawlette with a steady repeat to keep you engaged while it grows into shape. Worked in natural undyed wool, this versatile shawl will be easy to pair with other colors in your closet. The narrow size makes it perfect for days when just a touch of warmth will do.

TIMELINE

By knitting approximately 100 yards (91 m or about ¼ skein) a day, you can finish Walkabout in about 5 days with time left for blocking before the week ends.

CONSTRUCTION

Worked side to side in a crescent shape with increases on both the right side and wrong side rows (at the edges), your shawl will grow quickly in width without adding bulk to the body. You'll alternate sections of texture with stripes to keep things interesting along the way.

SKILL LEVEL

Intermediate

SIZE

One size fits most (see schematic for finished measurements)

MATERIALS

Yarn	• DK weight | Purl Soho Good Wool | 100% Andean highland wool, undyed | 383 yards (350 m) per 100 g skein | 500 yards (457 m) total • Color A: Hickory Nut, approximately 325 yards (297 m) • Color B: Driftwood Grey, approximately 175 yards (160 m) • Yarn substitutions may create different results. Please keep this in mind.
Needles	• U.S. size 8/5 mm (32" [80 cm]) circular needle
Gauge	• 16 st and 28 rows = 4" (10 cm) in pattern, blocked. Gauge is not essential.

MATERIALS

Notions	• Stitch markers • Darning needle to weave in ends

STITCH GLOSSARY

bet	between
BO	bind off
CO	cast on
dec	decrease
inc	increase
k	knit
k-yo-k	knit, yarn over, then knit again into the same st (2 st inc)
k2tog	knit 2 st together (dec 1)
k2togtbl	knit 2 st together through the back loop (dec 1)
ktbl	knit through the back loop
m	marker
p	purl
pm	place marker
psso	pass slipped st over
rem m	remove marker
rep	repeat
RS	right side
sl1	slip 1 st

(continued)

STITCH GLOSSARY

sm	slip marker
st	stitch/stitches
WS	wrong side
yo	yarn over (inc 1)

TIP: Watch for stitches in bold, a cue to a change in the stitch pattern.

WALKABOUT SHAWLETTE PATTERN

With U.S. size 8/5 mm (32" [80 cm]) circular needle and using Color A, CO 3 st using the cable cast-on method.

NOTE: The cable cast-on method starts your work on the right side immediately.

ROW 1 (RS): [K-yo-k] 3 times (9 st).

ROW 2 (WS): P1, yo, k to last st, yo, p1 (11 st).

ROW 3 (RS): K1, ktbl, k-yo-k, k5, k-yo-k, ktbl, k1 (15 st).

ROW 4 (WS): P1, yo, k to last st, yo, p1 (17 st).

ROW 5 (RS): K1, ktbl, k-yo-k, k to last 3 st, k-yo-k, ktbl, k1 (21 st).

ROW 6 (WS): Rep row 4 (23 st).

ROW 7 (RS): Rep row 5 (27 st).

ROW 8 (WS): Rep row 4 (29 st).

ROW 9 (RS): Rep row 5 (33 st).

ROW 10 (WS): Rep row 4 (35 st).

ROW 11 (RS): Rep row 5 (39 st).

ROW 12 (WS): Rep row 4 (41 st).

ROW 13 (RS): Rep row 5 (45 st).

ROW 14 (WS): Rep row 4 (47 st).

BEGIN SCALLOP

ROW 15 (RS): K1, ktbl, k-yo-k, pm, k1, [k2togtbl, k9, k2tog] rep bet brackets 2 times more (for a total of 3), k1, pm, k-yo-k, ktbl, k1 (do not count st this row).

ROW 16 (WS): P1, yo, p to last st, slipping markers as you go, yo, p1.

ROW 17 (RS): K1, ktbl, k-yo-k, k to m, sm, k1, [k2togtbl, k7, k2tog] rep bet brackets 2 times more (for a total of 3), k1, sm, k to last 3 st, k-yo-k, ktbl, k1 (do not count st this row).

ROW 18 (WS): P1, yo, p to last st, slipping markers as you go, yo, p1 (do not count st this row).

ROW 19 (RS): K1, ktbl, k-yo-k, k to m, sm, k1, [k2togtbl, yo, (k1, yo) 5 times, k2tog] rep bet brackets 2 times more (for a total of 3), k1, sm, k to last 3 st, k-yo-k, ktbl, k1 (63 st)—cut Color A.

WITH COLOR B

ROW 20 (WS): P1, yo, **k** to last st, yo, p1 (65 st).

ROW 21 (RS): K1, ktbl, k-yo-k, k to last 3 st, k-yo-k, ktbl, k1 (69 st).

ROW 22 (WS): P1, yo, p to last st, yo, p1 (71 st)—remove markers as you work this row.

ROW 23 (RS): K1, ktbl, k-yo-k, pm, [k2togtbl, k9, k2tog] rep bet brackets 4 more times (for a total of 5), pm, k-yo-k, ktbl, k1 (do not count st this row).

ROW 24 (WS): P1, yo, p to last st, yo, p1.

ROW 25 (RS): K1, ktbl, k-yo-k, k to m, sm, [k2togtbl, k7, k2tog] rep bet brackets to m, sm, k to last 3 st, k-yo-k, ktbl, k1 (do not count st this row).

ROW 26 (WS): P1, yo, p to last st, yo, p1.

ROW 27 (RS): K1, ktbl, k-yo-k, k to m, sm, [k2togtbl, yo, (k1, yo) 5 times, k2tog] rep bet brackets to m, sm, k to last 3 st, k-yo-k, ktbl, k1 (87 st)—cut Color B.

WITH COLOR A

ROW 28 (WS): P1, yo, **k** to last st, yo, p1 (89 st).

ROW 29 (RS): K1, ktbl, k-yo-k, k to m, sm, k to m, sm, k to last 3 st, k-yo-k, ktbl, k1 (93 st).

ROW 30 (WS): P1, yo, p to last st, yo, p1 (95 st)—remove markers as you work this row.

ROW 31 (RS): K1, ktbl, k-yo-k, pm, k1, k9, k2tog, [k2togtbl, k9, k2tog] rep bet brackets to last 15 st, k2togtbl, k9, k1, pm, k-yo-k, ktbl, k1 (do not count st this row).

ROW 32 (WS): P1, yo, p to last st, yo, p1 (89 st).

ROW 33 (RS): K1, ktbl, k-yo-k, k to 2 st before m, k2tog, sm, [k2togtbl, k7, k2tog] to m, sm, k2togtbl, k to last 3 st, k-yo-k, ktbl, k1 (do not count st this row).

ROW 34 (WS): P1, yo, p to last st, yo, p1 (83 st).

ROW 35 (RS): K1, ktbl, k-yo-k, k to 3 st before m, k1, yo, k2tog, rem m, [k2togtbl, yo, (k1, yo) 5 times, k2tog] rep bet brackets to m, rem m, k2togtbl, yo, k1, yo, k to last 3 st, k-yo-k, ktbl, k1 (111 st)—remove markers as you work this row.

GARTER (CONTINUE IN COLOR A UNTIL OTHERWISE STATED)

ROW 36 (WS): P1, yo, **k** to last st, yo, p1 (113 st).

ROW 37 (RS): K1, ktbl, k-yo-k, k to last 3 st, k-yo-k, ktbl, k1 (117 st).

REP rows 36 and 37 once more (123 st).

SCALLOP

ROW 40 (WS): P1, yo, **k** to last st, yo, p1 (125 st).

ROW 41 (RS): K1, ktbl, k-yo-k, pm, [k2togtbl, k9, k2tog] rep brackets 8 times more (for a total of 9), pm, k-yo-k, ktbl, k1 (do not count st this row).

ROW 42 (WS): P1, yo, p to last st, slipping markers as you go, yo, p1 (do not count st this row).

ROW 43 (RS): K1, ktbl, k-yo-k, k to m, sm, k1, [k2togtbl, k7, k2tog] rep bet brackets 8 times more (for a total of 9), k1, sm, k to last 3 st, k-yo-k, ktbl, k1 (do not count st this row).

ROW 44 (WS): P1, yo, p to last st, yo, p1 (do not count st this row).

ROW 45 (RS): K1, ktbl, k-yo-k, k to m, sm, k1, [k2togtbl, yo, (k1, yo) 5 times, k2tog] rep bet brackets 8 times more (for a total of 9), k1, sm, k to last 3 st, k-yo-k, ktbl, k1 (141 st)—cut Color A and remove markers as you work this row.

WITH COLOR B

ROW 46 (WS): P1, yo, **k** to last st, yo, p1 (143 st).

ROW 47 (RS): K1, ktbl, k-yo-k, k to last 3 st, k-yo-k, ktbl, k1 (147 st).

ROW 48 (WS): P1, yo, p to last st, yo, p1 (149 st).

ROW 49 (RS): K1, ktbl, k-yo-k, pm, [k2togtbl, k9, k2tog] to last 3 st, pm, k-yo-k, ktbl, k1 (do not count st this row).

ROW 50 (WS): P1, yo, p to last st, yo, p1 (do not count st this row).

ROW 51 (RS): K1, ktbl, k-yo-k, k to m, sm, [k2togtbl, k7, k2tog] to m, sm, k to last 3 st, k-yo-k, ktbl, k1 (115 st).

ROW 52 (WS): P1, yo, p to last st, yo, p1 (117 st).

ROW 53 (RS): K1, ktbl, k-yo-k, k to m, sm, [k2togtbl, yo, (k1, yo) 5 times, k2tog] to m, sm, k to last 3 st, k-yo-k, ktbl, k1 (165 st)—cut Color B.

WITH COLOR A

ROW 54 (WS): P1, yo, **k** to last st, yo, p1 (167 st).

GARTER (CONTINUE IN COLOR A UNTIL OTHERWISE STATED)

ROW 62 (WS): P1, yo, **k** to last st, yo, p1 (195 st).

ROW 63 (RS): K1, ktbl, k-yo-k, k to last 3 st, k-yo-k, ktbl, k1 (199 st).

REP these 2 rows once (205 st).

SCALLOP (WITH COLOR A)

ROW 66 (WS): P1, yo, **k** to last st, yo, p1 (207 st).

ROW 67 (RS): K1, ktbl, k-yo-k, k2, pm, k1, [k2togtbl, k9, k2tog] rep bet brackets 14 times more (for a total of 15), k1, pm, k2, k-yo-k, ktbl, k1 (do not count st this row).

ROW 68 (WS): P1, yo, p to last st, slipping markers as you go, yo, p1 (do not count st this row).

ROW 69 (RS): K1, ktbl, k-yo-k, k to m, sm, k1, [k2togtbl, k7, k2tog] rep bet brackets 14 times more (for a total of 15), k1, sm, k to last 3 st, k-yo-k, ktbl, k1 (do not count st this row).

ROW 70 (WS): P1, yo, p to last st, yo, p1 (do not count st this row).

ROW 71 (RS): K1, ktbl, k-yo-k, k to m, sm, k1, [k2togtbl, yo, (k1, yo) 5 times, k2tog] rep bet brackets 14 times more (for a total of 15), k1, sm, k to last 3 st, k-yo-k, ktbl, k1 (223 st)—cut Color A and remove markers as you work this row.

WITH COLOR B

ROW 72 (WS): P1, yo, **k** to last st, yo, p1 (225 st).

ROW 73 (RS): K1, ktbl, k-yo-k, k to last 3 st, k-yo-k, ktbl, k1 (229 st).

ROW 74 (WS): P1, yo, p to last st, yo, p1 (231 st).

ROW 75 (RS): K1, ktbl, k-yo-k, k2, pm, [k2togtbl, k9, k2tog] to last 3 st, pm, k2, k-yo-k, ktbl, k1 (do not count st this row).

ROW 76 (WS): P1, yo, p to last st, yo, p1 (do not count st this row).

ROW 77 (RS): K1, ktbl, k-yo-k, k to m, sm, [k2togtbl, k7, k2tog] to m, sm, k to last 3 st, k-yo-k, ktbl, k1 (do not count st this row).

ROW 78 (WS): P1, yo, p to last st, yo, p1 (do not count st this row).

ROW 79 (RS): K1, ktbl, k-yo-k, k to m, sm, [k2togtbl, yo, (k1, yo) 5 times, k2tog] to m, sm, k to last 3 st, k-yo-k, ktbl, k1 (247 st)—cut Color B.

ROW 55 (RS): K1, ktbl, k-yo-k, k to m, sm, k to m, sm, k to last 3 st, k-yo-k, ktbl, k1 (171 st).

ROW 56 (WS): P1, yo, p to last st, yo, p1 (173 st)—remove markers as you work this row.

ROW 57 (RS): K1, ktbl, k-yo-k, pm, k10, k2tog, [k2togtbl, k9, k2tog] to last 15 st, k2togtbl, k10, pm, k-yo-k, ktbl, k1 (do not count st this row).

ROW 58 (WS): P1, yo, p to last st, yo, p1 (do not count st this row).

ROW 59 (RS): K1, ktbl, k-yo-k, k to 2 st before m, k2tog, sm, [k2togtbl, k7, k2tog] to m, sm, k2togtbl, k to last 3 st, k-yo-k, ktbl, k1 (do not count st this row).

ROW 60 (WS): P1, yo, p to last st, yo, p1 (do not count st this row).

ROW 61 (RS): K1, ktbl, k-yo-k, k to 4 st before m, yo, k1, yo, k1, yo, k2tog, sm, [k2togtbl, yo (k1, yo) 5 times, k2tog] to m, sm, k2togtbl, yo, k1, yo, k1, yo, k to last 3 st, k-yo-k, ktbl, k1 (193 st)—remove markers as you work this row.

WITH COLOR A

ROW 80 (WS): P1, yo, **k** to last st, yo, p1 (249 st).

ROW 81 (RS): K1, ktbl, k-yo-k, k to m, sm, k to m, sm, k to last 3 st, k-yo-k, ktbl, k1 (253 st).

ROW 82 (WS): P1, yo, p to last st, yo, p1 (255 st)—remove markers as you work this row.

ROW 83 (RS): K1, ktbl, k-yo-k, k1, pm, [k2togtbl, k9, k2tog] to last 4 st, pm, k1, k-yo-k, ktbl, k1 (do not count st this row).

ROW 84 (WS): P1, yo, p to last st, yo, p1 (do not count st this row).

ROW 85 (RS): K1, ktbl, k-yo-k, k2, k2tog, sm, [k2togtbl, k7, k2tog] to m, sm, k2togtbl, k2, k-yo-k, ktbl, k1 (do not count st this row).

ROW 86 (WS): P1, yo, p to last st, yo, p1 (do not count st this row).

ROW 87 (RS): K1, ktbl, k-yo-k, k2, yo, k1, yo, k1, yo, k2tog, sm [k2togtbl, yo, (k1, yo) 5 times, k2tog] to m, sm, k2togtbl, yo, k1, yo, k1, yo, k2, k-yo-k, ktbl, k1 (273 st).

GARTER (CONTINUING IN COLOR A)

ROW 88 (WS): P1, yo, **k** to last st, yo, p1 (275 st).

ROW 89 (RS): K1, ktbl, k-yo-k, k to last 3 st, k-yo-k, ktbl, k1 (279 st).

REP these 2 rows twice more. On the next row, BO loosely (or use a stretchy bind-off) in k (291 st).

TIP: For a larger shawlette, repeat rows 88 and 89 until desired width, alternating colors every 2 rows (if desired).

WEAVE IN ends and wet block, pinning flat and drawing the top edge flat and taut along the blocking mat. Use blocking pins to draw out the curves of the scallops to help shape the shawl and to open the stitch pattern. The shawl will grow and relax significantly with blocking.

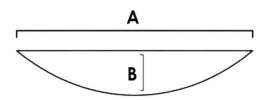

FINISHED MEASUREMENTS

A: 55" (140 cm) wide

B: 10" (25 cm) tall

May Day Shawl

May weather can be a bit unpredictable. Spring blooms and bold streams of sunlight always give me a false sense of security about the temperature outside; there's nothing quite like wearing your summer clothes a few weeks too early. The May Day Shawl celebrates the beauty of spring color while guarding against days that end up being chillier than expected. The texture repeat is ridiculously easy to memorize and so fun to knit you may want to cast on another one as soon as you finish!

TIMELINE

Knit in a medium-weight yarn on larger-than-usual needles, this open-texture shawl comes together very quickly. Knitting about 150 yards (137 m) per day (or ½ a skein of Color A and Color B per day), motivated knitters can finish in about 5 days with a few hours of knitting each day.

CONSTRUCTION

Knit diagonally from the side corner to the far edge, May Day is a steady, rhythmic project with all-over texture. The color changes are worked every second row once the pattern repeats begin, making it easy to switch between colors and to carry the second color up the side. This means you'll have fewer ends to weave in—quite a time-saver!

SKILL LEVEL

Intermediate

SIZE

One size fits most (see schematic for finished measurements)

MATERIALS

Yarn	• DK weight | Brooklyn Tweed Arbor | 100% Targhee wool | 145 yards (133 m) per 50 g skein | 4 skeins or 580 yards (530 m) total
	• Color A: Klimt 2 skeins or 290 yards (265 m)
	• Color B: Mesa 2 skeins or 290 yards (265 m)
	• Yarn substitutions may create different results. Please keep this in mind.
Needles	• U.S. size 8/5 mm (32" [80 cm]) circular needle

MATERIALS

Gauge	• 16 st and 23 rows = 4" (10 cm) in pattern, blocked (gauge is not critical)
Notions	• Locking stitch marker
	• Darning needle to weave in ends

STITCH GLOSSARY

[ ]	brackets always indicate a repeat
bet	between
BO	bind off
CO	cast on
k	knit
Inc	increase
kfb	knit into front and back of same st (inc 1)
p	purl
rep	repeat
RS	right side
WS	wrong side
yo	yarn over (inc 1)

MAY DAY SHAWL PATTERN

With U.S. size 8/5 mm (32" [80 cm]) circular needle and using Color A, CO 2 st using the cable cast-on method.

ROW 1 (RS): Kfb, k1 (3 st).

ROW 2 (WS): K.

NEXT ROW (WS): With Color B (for the first repeat series), p.

NEXT ROW (RS): With Color B (for the first repeat series), k1, kfb, [yo, k3—then pass the first of the 3 st over the other 2] to last st, k1 (1 st inc).

NEXT ROW (WS): With Color A (the first time through), p.

NEXT ROW (RS): With Color A (the first time through), k1, kfb, [yo, k3—then pass the first of the 3 st over the other 2] to last 2 st, k2 (1 st inc).

NEXT ROW (WS): With Color B (the first time through), p.

NEXT ROW (RS): With Color B (the first time through), k1, kfb, [yo, k3—then pass the first of the 3 st over the other 2] to last 3 st, k3 (1 st inc).

NOTE: Every time you start over working the Repeat Series, you will be starting with the opposite color that you started with the last time. It's easy to remember because you will switch to the other color every WS row, but you will continue to work the stitch pattern as written.

ROW 3 (RS): K1, kfb, k1 (attach a locking marker anywhere on this side to help keep track of the right side) (4 st).

ROW 4 (WS): K.

ROW 5 (RS): K1, kfb, k to end (5 st).

ROW 6 (WS): K.

ROW 7 (RS): K1, kfb, k to end (6 st).

REP rows 6 and 7 until you have 10 st.

WITH COLOR B (DO NOT CUT COLOR A)

NEXT ROW (WS): With Color B, p.

NEXT ROW (RS): With Color B, k1, kfb, [yo, k3—then pass the first of the 3 st over the other 2] rep bet brackets once, k2 (11 st).

NEXT ROW (WS): With Color A, p.

NEXT ROW (RS): With Color A, k1, kfb, [yo, k3—then pass the first of the 3 st over the other 2] rep bet brackets once, k3 (12 st).

CONTINUE to work the 6-row repeat series, alternating Color A and B every other row and increasing 1 st every RS row until you have 139 st and have finished a RS row. Change the color once more and work back on the WS row in pattern, then BO on the right side with medium loose tension (not too tight, not too loose). Wet block, pinned flat until dry.

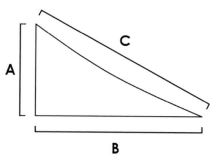

FINISHED MEASUREMENTS

A: 37" (94 cm)

B: 55" (140 cm)

C: 67" (170 cm)

Flower Girl Shawl

Rarely do you get the opportunity to combine three different weights of yarn into one project—now is your chance! This three-weights-in-one shawl is perfect for "stash diving" (using up those random, but lovely, single skeins you have sitting around). Two of the yarns are the same color, held double, but you could easily use different shades and play with the effect.

TIMELINE

Although not at all difficult, I recommend giving yourself the full week of knitting to savor every stitch.

CONSTRUCTION

Knit side to side from the smallest point to the widest edge, Flower Girl will delight your senses with color and texture. Using three different individual yarns adds to the visual and textural interest.

SKILL LEVEL

Intermediate

SIZE

One size fits most (see schematic for finished measurements)

MATERIALS

Yarn	• Fingering weight | Little Fox Yarn Monos | 100% superwash Merino | 400 yards (366 m) per 100 g skein | Color A: Tomato-Tomahto • Lace weight | Little Fox Yarn Little Mo | 72% kid mohair, 28% silk | 459 yards (420 m) per 50 g skein | Color B: Tomato-Tomahto • DK weight | Little Fox Yarn Bōsa | 65% superwash Merino, 20% silk, 15% yak | 231 yards (211 m) per 100 g skein | Color C: Natural • Note: Colors B and C are held double and worked together throughout the pattern. • Yarn substitutions may create different results. Please keep this in mind.
Needles	• U.S. size 7/4.5 mm (32" [80 cm]) circular needle
Gauge	• 16½ st and 24 rows = 4" (10 cm) in stockinette stitch

MATERIALS

Notions	• Cable needle • Stitch markers, including a locking marker • Darning needle to weave in ends

STITCH GLOSSARY

[ ]	brackets always indicate a repeat
bet	between
BO	bind off
CO	cast on
dec	decrease
inc	increase
k	knit
k2tog	knit 2 st together (dec 1)
kfb	knit into front and back of same stitch (inc 1)
p	purl
pm	place marker
rep	repeat
RS	right side
sl2wyib	slip 2 st to the right needle with yarn in back (do not knit them)
sl2wyif	slip 2 st to the right needle with yarn in front (do not knit them)
sm	slip marker
st	stitch/stitches
WS	wrong side

FLOWER GIRL SHAWL PATTERN

With U.S. size 7/4.5 mm (32" [80 cm]) circular needle and Color A, CO 2 st using any method.

ROW 1 (RS): Kfb, k1 (1 st inc).

ROW 2 (WS): K.

ROW 3 (RS): K1, kfb, k1 (attach a locking marker anywhere on this side to help keep track of the right side) (4 st).

ROW 4 (WS): K.

ROW 5 (RS): K1, kfb, k to end (1 st inc).

ROW 6 (WS): K.

REP rows 5 and 6 until you have 22 st.

PATTERN SERIES

ROW 1 (RS): K1, kfb, k to end (23 st).

ROW 2 (WS): K4, p2, [k5, p2] to last 3 st, k3.

ROW 3 (RS): With Color B/C (held double), k1, kfb, k1, pm, [sl2wyib, k5] to last 6 st, sl2wyib, k4 (24 st).

ROW 4 (WS): With Color B/C (held double), p4, [sl2wyif, p5] to last 6 st, sl2wyif, sm, p4.

ROW 5 (RS): With Color B/C (held double), k1, kfb, k2, sm, sl2wyib, [k5, sl2wyib] to last 4 st, k4 (25 st).

ROW 6 (WS): With Color B/C (held double), p4, [sl2wyif, p5] to last 7 st, sl2wyif, sm, p to end.

ROW 7 (RS): With Color A, k1, kfb, [k1, slip next 2 st to cable needle and hold to back of work, knit 1 (this is the first slipped st in Color A), k the 2 st from the cable needle, slip the next st (the second slipped st in Color A) to a cable needle and hold to front of work, knit the next 2 st on the left needle, then knit the st from the cable needle] rep bet brackets to last 2 st, k2 (26 st).

ROW 8 (WS): With Color A, k.

ROW 9 (RS): With Color B/C, k1, kfb, k to end (27 st).

ROW 10 (WS): With Color B/C, k.

ROW 11 (RS): With Color A, k1, kfb, k to end (28 st).

ROW 12 (WS): With Color A, k.

ROW 13 (RS): With Color B/C, k1, kfb, k to end (29 st).

ROW 14 (WS): With Color B/C, k.

REP the Pattern Series rows (in full) 10 times more (11 repeats in all). Begin the Pattern Series again, working only rows 1 through 8 (103 st). Cut Color A.

NEXT ROW (RS): With Color B/C, k1, kfb, k to end (104 st).

NEXT ROW (WS): With Color B/C, p.

REP these 2 rows 3 times in all (106 st).

JOIN Color A, but do not cut Color B/C.

NEXT ROW (RS): With Color A, k1, kfb, k to end (107 st).

NEXT ROW (WS): With Color A, k.

CUT Color A.

NEXT ROW (RS): With Color B/C, k1, kfb, k to end (108 st).

NEXT ROW (WS): With Color B/C, p.

REP these 2 rows 3 times in all (110 st).

JOIN Color A, but do not cut Color B/C.

NEXT ROW (RS): With Color A, k1, kfb, k to end (111 st).

NEXT ROW (WS): With Color A, k.

CUT Color A.

NEXT ROW (RS): With Color B/C, k1, kfb, k to end (112 st).

NEXT ROW (WS): With Color B/C, p.

REP these 2 rows 3 times in all (114 st).

JOIN Color A, but do not cut Color B/C.

START THE PATTERN SERIES AGAIN:

ROW 1 (RS): With Color A, k1, kfb, k to end (115 st).

ROW 2 (WS): With Color A, k4, [p2, k5] to last 6 st, p2, k4.

ROW 3 (RS): With Color B/C (held double), k1, kfb, k2, pm, [sl2wyib, k5] to last 6 st, sl2wyib, k4 (116 st).

ROW 4 (WS): With Color B/C (held double), p4, [sl2wyif, p5] to last 6 st, sl2wyif, sm, p4.

ROW 5 (RS): With Color B/C (held double), k1, kfb, k2, sm, [sl2wyib, k5] to last 6 st, sl2wyif, k4 (117 st).

ROW 6 (WS): With Color B/C (held double), p4, [sl2wyib, p5] to last 6 st, sl2wyib, sm, p to end.

ROW 7 (RS): With Color A, k1, kfb, k2, [k1, slip next 2 st to cable needle and hold to back of work, knit 1 (this is the first slipped st in Color A), k the 2 st from the cable needle, slip the next st (the second slipped st in Color A) to a cable needle and hold to front of work, knit the next 2 st on the left needle, then knit the st from the cable needle] rep bet brackets to last st, k1 (118 st).

ROW 8 (WS): With Color A, k.

ROW 9 (RS): With Color B, k1, kfb, k to end.

ROW 10 (WS): With Color B, k.

ROW 11 (RS): With Color A, k1, kfb, k to end.

ROW 12 (WS): With Color A, k.

ROW 13 (RS): With Color B, k1, kfb, k to end.

ROW 14 (WS): With Color B, k.

REP rows 1–14 of the Pattern Series once more. Then begin the series again, working only rows 1–8. Cut Color A.

NEXT ROW (RS): With Color B/C, k1, kfb, k to end.

NEXT ROW (WS): With Color B/C, p.

REP these 2 rows 3 times in all.

JOIN Color A, but do not cut Color B/C.

NEXT ROW (RS): With Color A, k1, kfb, k to end.

NEXT ROW (WS): With Color A, k to end.

CUT Color A.

NEXT ROW (RS): With Color B/C, k1, kfb, k to end.

NEXT ROW (WS): With Color B/C, p to end.

REP these 2 rows 3 times in all.

JOIN Color A, but do not cut Color B/C.

NEXT ROW (RS): With Color A, k1, kfb, k to end.

NEXT ROW (WS): With Color A, k.

CUT Color A.

NEXT ROW (RS): With Color B/C, k1, kfb, k to end.

NEXT ROW (WS): With Color B/C, p.

REP these 2 rows 3 times in all.

JOIN Color A, but do not cut Color B/C.

GARTER EDGE

NEXT ROW (RS): With Color A, k1, kfb, k to end.

NEXT ROW (WS): With Color A, k to end.

NEXT ROW (RS): With Color B/C, k1, kfb, k to end.

NEXT ROW (WS): With Color B/C, k to end.

NEXT ROW (RS): With Color A, k1, kfb, k to end.

NEXT ROW (WS): With Color A, k to end.

NEXT ROW (RS): With Color B/C, k1, kfb, k to end.

NEXT ROW (WS): With Color B/C, k to end.

NEXT ROW (RS): With Color A, k1, kfb, k to end. Remove markers as you go.

NEXT ROW (WS): With Color A, BO as you knit across this final row with medium loose tension.

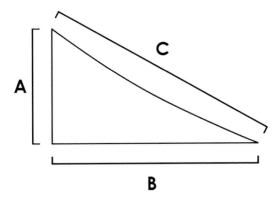

FINISHED MEASUREMENTS

A: 38" (97 cm)

B: 46" (117 cm)

C: 53" (135 cm)

Puddlejumper Shawl

My goal for Puddlejumper was to create a shawl that was lightweight, effortless and—above all else—quick to knit. The end result surprised me, not just because it fit my criteria perfectly, but also because I absolutely loved wearing it. It quickly became my favorite accessory in the warm season. Puddlejumper is the perfect lightweight layer on a spring day. Inspired by blooming flowers and spring puddles, this easy-breezy shawl will be an instant favorite.

TIMELINE

At a pace of approximately 150 yards (137 m or just ½ skein) a day (which will go quickly given the stitch pattern), most knitters can knit this quick shawl in about 3 days of easy knitting.

CONSTRUCTION

Knit bottom-up from the center tip to the top edge at a loose gauge, Puddlejumper is a delicate, lightweight knit for warmer weather. The tassel is added afterward with remaining yarn and adds a perfect final touch to the shawl.

SKILL LEVEL

Advanced Beginner

SIZE

One size fits most (see schematic for finished measurements)

MATERIALS

Yarn	• Light worsted weight | Purl Soho Understory | 50% baby alpaca, 25% baby yak, 25% silk | 250 yards (229 m) per 100 g skein | 450 yards (411 m) total (1 full skein MC, 1 partial skein CC)
	• Main Color (MC): Pink Earth 1 skein or 250 yards (229 m)
	• Contrast Color (CC): Willow Bark 1 partial skein or 200 yards (183 m)
	• Yarn substitutions may create different results. Please keep this in mind.
Needles	• U.S. size 10/6 mm (32" [80 cm]) circular needle

MATERIALS

Gauge	• 10 st and 24 rows = 4" (10 cm) in stockinette stitch (blocked) when worked between rows of the drop-stitch pattern (which draws the stitch gauge out widthwise). Gauge is not essential, but should be light and loose.
Notions	• Darning needle to weave in ends

STITCH GLOSSARY

[ ]	brackets always indicate a repeat
BO	bind off
CC	contrast color
CO	cast on
k	knit
kfb	knit into front and back of same st (inc 1)
MC	main color
p	purl
rep	repeat
RS	right side
st	stitch/stitches
WS	wrong side

PUDDLEJUMPER SHAWL PATTERN

With U.S. size 10/6 mm (32" [80 cm]) circular needle and MC, CO 3 st.

ROW 1 (RS): Kfb, kfb, k1 (5 st).

NEXT ROW WITH CC (RS): K1, kfb, [k (wrapping yarn twice for each st)] to last 3 st, kfb, k2.

NEXT ROW WITH CC (WS): K across, dropping the extra wraps as you work each st.

NEXT ROW WITH CC (RS): K1, kfb, [k (wrapping yarn twice for each st)] to last 3 st, kfb, k2.

CUT CC. Join MC on the WS and p across the row.

NEXT ROW WITH MC (RS): K1, kfb, k to 3 st before end, kfb, k2. Note: you will drop the extra wraps as you go.

NEXT ROW WITH MC (WS): P2, k1, p to last 3 st, k1, p2.

REP these 2 rows 2 times more (for a total of 3).

REP the Pattern Repeat Series 12 more times (for a total of 13—you should have 13 drop-stitch ridges in the contrast color when you have finished). BO in the MC on the RS as you k across.

TIP: Because of the loose gauge, be extra careful about weaving in your ends to ensure they do not come loose.

WET BLOCK and lay flat to dry. The pattern should flatten and expand significantly with blocking.

USE the remaining yarn to create a tassel (see page 145 for instructions) and attach it to the bottom center tip of the shawl.

ROW 2 (WS): P1, k1, p1, k1, p1.

ROW 3 (RS): K1, kfb, kfb, k2 (7 st).

ROW 4 (WS): P2, k1, p1, k1, p2.

ROW 5 (RS): K1, kfb, k2, kfb, k2 (9 st).

ROW 6 (WS): P2, k1, p3, k1, p2.

ROW 7 (RS): K1, kfb, k4, kfb, k2 (11 st).

ROW 8 (WS): P2, k1, p5, k1, p2.

ROW 9 (RS): K1, kfb, k to 3 st before end, kfb, k2 (13 st).

ROW 10 (WS): P2, k1, p to last 3 st, k1, p2.

REP rows 9 and 10 until you have 17 st.

PATTERN REPEAT SERIES

CUT MC, leaving a tail*. Join CC.

*When cutting or joining colors, always leave a tail at least 4" (10 cm) long to weave in later.

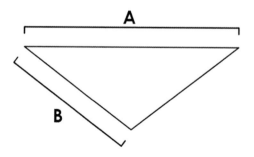

FINISHED MEASUREMENTS

A: 52" (132 cm) wide

B: 32" (80 cm) top to bottom

Smooth stockinette and charming flower buds combine for a sweet, lightweight wrap to wear around your shoulders on a spring day. It also works beautifully as a long cowl to wear in cooler months. The repeats will become second-nature in no time, making it the ideal project for social knitting. Don't skip the blocking process—you'll be amazed at how it enhances the pattern and encourages drape.

TIMELINE

At a pace of about ½ skein (or about 110 yards [101 m]) per day, you can finish your Darling Bud Wrap in 4 to 5 days. Give yourself an extra day for grafting and blocking, and you'll be ready to wear your wrap by the next weekend!

CONSTRUCTION

Knit back and forth (flat) as one long rectangle, Darling Bud is joined together at the end with a decorative grafting technique.

SKILL LEVEL

Advanced Beginner

SIZE

One size fits most (see schematic for finished measurements)

MATERIALS

Yarn	• Light worsted weight | Purl Soho Flax Down | 43% baby alpaca, 42% extra fine Merino, 15% linen | 219 yards (200 m) per 100 g skein | 2 skeins or 438 yards (400 m) total • Color: Rose Granite
Needles	• U.S. size 7/4.5 mm (24-32" [60-80 cm]) circular needle • U.S. size E (3.5 mm) crochet hook
Gauge	• 16½ st and 25 rows = 4" (10 cm) in pattern stitch, blocked
Notions	• Stitch markers • Darning needle to weave in ends

STITCH GLOSSARY

[ ]	brackets always indicate a repeat
bet	between
BO	bind off
CO	cast on
dec	decrease
inc	increase
k	knit
rep	repeat
RS	right side
s2kp2	slip 2 st as if to knit, k the next st on the left needle, then pass the 2 slipped st over (dec 2)
st	stitch/stitches
WS	wrong side
yo	yarn over (inc 1)

DARLING BUD WRAP PATTERN

With U.S. size 7/4.5 mm (24-32" [60-80 cm]) circular needle, CO 83 st using a provisional cast-on (see page 146).

SET-UP ROW 1 (RS): K.

SET-UP ROW 2 (WS): P.

DARLING BUD PATTERN REPEAT

ROW 1 (RS): K4, [yo, s2kp2, yo, k3] to end, ending final rep with k4 instead of k3.

ROW 2 (WS): P.

ROW 3 (RS): K1, [yo, s2kp2, yo, k3] to end, ending final rep with yo, k1 instead of yo, k3.

ROW 4 (WS): P.

ROW 5 (RS): Rep row 1.

ROW 6 (WS): P.

ROW 7 (RS): Rep row 3.

ROW 8 (WS): P.

ROW 9 (RS): Rep row 1.

ROW 10 (WS): P.

ROW 11 (RS): Rep row 3.

ROW 12 (WS): P.

ROW 13, 15, 17 (RS): K.

ROW 14, 16, 18 (WS): P.

REP rows 1–18 until the wrap measures 35" (89 cm) long. If you prefer a wider circumference for your desired fit, continue to add length until the wrap fits nicely around your upper shoulders and body.

END with a stockinette series (Rows 13–18). Do not bind off.

REMOVE the provisional cast-on and place the original live st onto your needle to prepare for grafting. Graft together the live st from the cast-on and the final row using either Kitchener stitch or Russian Grafting (see page 146 for Russian Grafting technique).

WET BLOCK, pinning the edges flat and smooth, until dry.

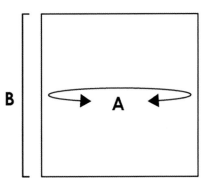

FINISHED MEASUREMENTS

A: 35" (89 cm) long, prior to joining

B: 20" (51 cm) top to bottom

Thunderstorm Shawl

There's nothing I love more than a thunderstorm; the percussion in the air sends a little wave of excitement through our home. Growing up in the Midwest, we had our share of wicked spring storms and I always found them quite exciting. Even now, we will hunker down near the fire, get our candles ready (just in case) and listen to the storm until it passes. It feels a bit magical. The electric zigs and zags of "lightning" paired with horizontal ridges in this shawl are my nod to the greyest, rainiest days when we are fortunate enough to hear the skies roar.

TIMELINE

Although the shawl itself is quite large, the repeats are fairly easy to follow without significant focus. Knitters with a few hours available each day can finish this project in about 7 days by knitting approximately 100 yards (91 m or approximately 1 ball) per day.

CONSTRUCTION

Knit side-to-side from the smallest point to the longest wave panel, Thunderstorm is worked with increases every right side row along one edge. Don't let the length of the pattern deter you; the process is quite simple and will be easy to repeat. The rows are written out to make it easier for you to avoid having to refer back to previous pages to see how a repeat is worked. The process creates a long, thin shawl that gradually grows along just one side. Intermittent wave stitches (a nod to falling rain) are offset by garter ridges, with shades of grey alternating throughout the pattern. You'll be changing colors on alternating rows, which means there is no official right side, and you'll see little "zigs" from the color changes on both sides.

SKILL LEVEL

Advanced Beginner

SIZE

One size fits most (see schematic for finished measurements)

MATERIALS

Yarn	• DK weight | HiKoo Llamor | 100% baby alpaca | 109 yards (100 m) per 50 g ball | 6 balls or 654 yards (598 m) total
	• Main Color (MC): Stone 3 balls or 327 yards (299 m)
	• Contrast Color (CC): Coal 3 balls or 327 yards (299 m)
	• Yarn substitutions may create different results. Please keep this in mind.
Needles	• U.S. size 8/5 mm (32" [80 cm]) circular needle
Gauge	• 17 st and 16 rows = 4" (10 cm) in garter stitch, blocked
	• 16 st and 26 rows = 4" (10 cm) in lace pattern, blocked
Notions	• Locking stitch marker
	• Darning needle to weave in ends

STITCH GLOSSARY

[ ]	brackets always indicate a repeat
bet	between
BO	bind off
CC	contrast color
CO	cast on
dec	decrease
inc	increase
k	knit
k2tog	knit 2 st together (dec 1)

(continued)

STITCH GLOSSARY

kfb	knit into front and back of same st (inc 1)
MC	main color
p	purl
rep	repeat
RS	right side
ssk	slip, slip, knit 2 together (dec 1)
st	stitch/stitches
WS	wrong side
yo	yarn over (inc 1)

NOTE: For a tidy edge, pull the working yarn nice and tight after you work the first stitch. It helps to do this by inserting the needle into the second stitch, then pull the working yarn tight (it will tighten up the first stitch when you do this), then work the stitch—and the remaining stitches on the row—as usual.

THUNDERSTORM SHAWL PATTERN

With U.S. size 8/5 mm (32" [80 cm]) circular needle and MC (dark grey), and using your preferred cast-on method, CO 2 st.

ROW 1 (RS): Kfb, k1 (3 st).

ROW 2 (WS): P.

ROW 3 (RS): K1, kfb, k1 (attach a locking marker anywhere on this side to help keep track of the right side) (4 st).

ROW 4 (WS): P.

ROW 5 (RS): K1, kfb, k to end (5 st).

ROW 6 (WS): K3, p2.

ROW 7 (RS): K1, kfb, k to end (6 st).

ROW 8 (WS): K3, p to end.

REP rows 7 and 8 until you have 24 st, ending after a RS row.

NEXT ROW (WS): Join CC, k3, p to end.

NEXT ROW (RS): With CC, k1, kfb, k1, [k2tog] 3 times, [yo, k1] 5 times, yo, [ssk] 3 times, k4 (25 st).

NEXT ROW (WS): With CC, k3, p to end.

NEXT ROW (RS): With CC, k1, kfb, k to end (26 st).

NEXT ROW (WS): With MC, k3, p to end.

NEXT ROW (RS): With MC, k1, kfb, k1, [k2tog] 3 times, [yo, k1] 5 times, yo, [ssk] 3 times, k to end (27 st).

NEXT ROW (WS): With MC, k3, p to end.

NEXT ROW (RS): With MC, k1, kfb, k to end (28 st).

NEXT ROW (WS): Join CC, k3, p to end.

NEXT ROW (RS): With CC, k1, kfb, k1, [k2tog] 3 times, [yo, k1] 5 times, yo, [ssk] 3 times, k to end (29 st).

NEXT ROW (WS): With CC, k3, p to end.

NEXT ROW (RS): With CC, k1, kfb, k to end (30 st).

NEXT ROW (WS): With MC, k across.

NEXT ROW (RS): With MC, k1, kfb, k to end (31 st).

NEXT ROW (WS): With MC, k across.

NEXT ROW (RS): With MC, k1, kfb, k to end (32 st).

NEXT ROW (WS): With CC, k across.

NEXT ROW (RS): With CC, k1, kfb, k to end (33 st).

NEXT ROW (WS): With CC, k across.

NEXT ROW (RS): With CC, k1, kfb, k to end (34 st).

NEXT ROW (WS): With MC, k across.

NEXT ROW (RS): With MC, k1, kfb, k to end (35 st).

NEXT ROW (WS): With MC, k across.

NEXT ROW (RS): With MC, k1, kfb, k to end (36 st).

NEXT ROW (WS): With CC, k across.

NEXT ROW (RS): With CC, k1, kfb, k to end (37 st).

NEXT ROW (WS): With CC, k across.

NEXT ROW (RS): With CC, k1, kfb, k to end (38 st).

NEXT ROW (WS): With MC, k across.

NEXT ROW (RS): With MC, k1, kfb, k to end (39 st).

NEXT ROW (WS): With MC, k across.

NEXT ROW (RS): With MC, k1, kfb, k to end (40 st).

NEXT ROW (WS): With CC, k across.

NEXT ROW (RS): With CC, k1, kfb, k to end (41 st).

NEXT ROW (WS): With CC, k across.

NEXT ROW (RS): With CC, k1, kfb, k to end (42 st).

NEXT ROW (WS): With MC, k across.

NEXT ROW (RS): With MC, k1, kfb, k to end (43 st).

NEXT ROW (WS): With MC, k across.

NEXT ROW (RS): With MC, k1, kfb, k to end (44 st).

NEXT ROW (WS): With CC, k across.

NEXT ROW (RS): With CC, k1, kfb, k to end (45 st).

NEXT ROW (WS): With CC, k across.

NEXT ROW (RS): With CC, k1, kfb, k to end (46 st).

NEXT ROW (WS): With MC, k3, p to end.

NEXT ROW (RS): With MC, k1, kfb, k1, [(k2tog) 3 times, (yo, k1) 5 times, yo, (ssk) 3 times] rep bet brackets once more, k to end (47 st).

NEXT ROW (WS): With MC, k3, p to end.

NEXT ROW (RS): With MC, k1, kfb, k to end (48 st).

NEXT ROW (WS): Join CC, k3, p to end.

NEXT ROW (RS): With CC, k1, kfb, k1, [(k2tog) 3 times, (yo, k1) 5 times, yo, (ssk) 3 times] rep bet brackets once more, k to end (49 st).

NEXT ROW (WS): With CC, k3, p to end.

NEXT ROW (RS): With CC, k1, kfb, k to end (50 st).

NEXT ROW (WS): With MC, k3, p to end.

NEXT ROW (RS): With MC, k1, kfb, k1, [(k2tog) 3 times, (yo, k1) 5 times, yo, (ssk) 3 times] rep bet brackets once more, k to end (51 st).

NEXT ROW (WS): With MC, k3, p to end.

NEXT ROW (RS): With MC, k1, kfb, k to end (52 st).

NEXT ROW (WS): With CC, k across.

NEXT ROW (RS): With CC, k1, kfb, k to end (53 st).

NEXT ROW (WS): With CC, k across.

NEXT ROW (RS): With CC, k1, kfb, k to end (54 st).

NEXT ROW (WS): With MC, k across.

NEXT ROW (RS): With MC, k1, kfb, k to end (55 st).

NEXT ROW (WS): With MC, k across.

NEXT ROW (RS): With MC, k1, kfb, k to end (56 st).

NEXT ROW (WS): With CC, k across.

NEXT ROW (RS): With CC, k1, kfb, k to end (57 st).

NEXT ROW (WS): With CC, k across.

NEXT ROW (RS): With CC, k1, kfb, k to end (58 st).

NEXT ROW (WS): With MC, k across.

NEXT ROW (RS): With MC, k1, kfb, k to end (59 st).

NEXT ROW (WS): With MC, k across.

NEXT ROW (RS): With MC, k1, kfb, k to end (60 st).

NEXT ROW (WS): With CC, k across.

NEXT ROW (RS): With CC, k1, kfb, k to end (61 st).

NEXT ROW (WS): With CC, k across.

NEXT ROW (RS): With CC, k1, kfb, k to end (62 st).

NEXT ROW (WS): With MC, k across.

NEXT ROW (RS): With MC, k1, kfb, k to end (63 st).

NEXT ROW (WS): With MC, k across.

NEXT ROW (RS): With MC, k1, kfb, k to end (64 st).

NEXT ROW (WS): With CC, k across.

NEXT ROW (RS): With CC, k1, kfb, k to end (65 st).

NEXT ROW (WS): With CC, k across.

NEXT ROW (RS): With CC, k1, kfb, k to end (66 st).

NEXT ROW (WS): With MC, k across.

NEXT ROW (RS): With MC, k1, kfb, k to end (67 st).

NEXT ROW (WS): With MC, k across.

NEXT ROW (RS): With MC, k1, kfb, k to end (68 st).

NEXT ROW (WS): With CC, k3, p to end.

NEXT ROW (RS): With CC, k1, kfb, k1, [(k2tog) 3 times, (yo, k1) 5 times, yo, (ssk) 3 times], rep bet brackets twice more, k to end (69 st).

NEXT ROW (WS): With CC, k3, p to end.

NEXT ROW (RS): With CC, k1, kfb, k to end (70 st).

NEXT ROW (WS): With MC, k3, p to end.

NEXT ROW (RS): With MC, k1, kfb, k1, [(k2tog) 3 times, (yo, k1) 5 times, yo, (ssk) 3 times] rep bet brackets twice more, k to end (71 st).

NEXT ROW (WS): With MC, k3, p to end.

NEXT ROW (RS): With MC, k1, kfb, k to end (72 st).

NEXT ROW (WS): With CC, k3, p to end.

NEXT ROW (RS): With CC, k1, kfb, k1, [(k2tog) 3 times, (yo, k1) 5 times, yo, (ssk) 3 times] rep bet brackets twice more, k to end (73 st).

NEXT ROW (WS): With CC, k3, p to end.

NEXT ROW (RS): With CC, k1, kfb, k to end (74 st).

NEXT ROW (WS): With MC, k across.

NEXT ROW (RS): With MC, k1, kfb, k to end (75 st).

NEXT ROW (WS): With MC, k across.

NEXT ROW (RS): With MC, k1, kfb, k to end (76 st).

NEXT ROW (WS): With CC, k across.

NEXT ROW (RS): With CC, k1, kfb, k to end (77 st).

NEXT ROW (WS): With CC, k across.

NEXT ROW (RS): With CC, k1, kfb, k to end (78 st).

NEXT ROW (WS): With MC, k across.

NEXT ROW (RS): With MC, k1, kfb, k to end (79 st).

NEXT ROW (WS): With MC, k across.

NEXT ROW (RS): With MC, k1, kfb, k to end (80 st).

NEXT ROW (WS): With CC, k across.

NEXT ROW (RS): With CC, k1, kfb, k to end (81 st).

NEXT ROW (WS): With CC, k across.

NEXT ROW (RS): With CC, k1, kfb, k to end (82 st).

NEXT ROW (WS): With MC, k across.

NEXT ROW (RS): With MC, k1, kfb, k to end (83 st).

NEXT ROW (WS): With MC, k across.

NEXT ROW (RS): With MC, k1, kfb, k to end (84 st).

NEXT ROW (WS): With CC, k across.

NEXT ROW (RS): With CC, k1, kfb, k to end (85 st).

NEXT ROW (WS): With CC, k across.

NEXT ROW (RS): With CC, k1, kfb, k to end (86 st).

NEXT ROW (WS): With MC, k across.

NEXT ROW (RS): With MC, k1, kfb, k to end (87 st).

NEXT ROW (WS): With MC, k across.

NEXT ROW (RS): With MC, k1, kfb, k to end (88 st).

NEXT ROW (WS): With CC, k across.

NEXT ROW (RS): With CC, k1, kfb, k to end (89 st).

NEXT ROW (WS): With CC, k across.

NEXT ROW (RS): With CC, k1, kfb, k to end (90 st).

NEXT ROW (WS): With MC, k3, p to end.

NEXT ROW (RS): With MC, k1, kfb, k1, [(k2tog) 3 times, (yo, k1) 5 times, yo, (ssk) 3 times] rep bet brackets 3 times more, k to end (91 st).

NEXT ROW (WS): With MC, k3, p to end.

NEXT ROW (RS): With MC, k1, kfb, k to end (92 st).

NEXT ROW (WS): With CC, k3, p to end.

NEXT ROW (RS): With CC, k1, kfb, k1, [(k2tog) 3 times, (yo, k1) 5 times, yo, (ssk) 3 times] rep bet brackets 3 times more, k to end (93 st).

NEXT ROW (WS): With CC, k3, p to end.

NEXT ROW (RS): With CC, k1, kfb, k to end (94 st).

NEXT ROW (WS): With MC, k3, p to end.

NEXT ROW (RS): With MC, k1, kfb, k1, [(k2tog) 3 times, (yo, k1) 5 times, yo, (ssk) 3 times] rep bet brackets 3 times more, k to end (95 st).

NEXT ROW (WS): With MC, k3, p to end.

NEXT ROW (RS): With MC, k1, kfb, k to end (96 st).

NEXT ROW (WS): With CC, k across.

NEXT ROW (RS): With CC, k1, kfb, k to end (97 st).

NEXT ROW (WS): With CC, k across.

NEXT ROW (RS): With CC, k1, kfb, k to end (98 st).

NEXT ROW (WS): With MC, k across.

NEXT ROW (RS): With MC, k1, kfb, k to end (99 st).

NEXT ROW (WS): With MC, k across.

NEXT ROW (RS): With MC, k1, kfb, k to end (100 st).

NEXT ROW (WS): With CC, k across.

NEXT ROW (RS): With CC, k1, kfb, k to end (101 st).

NEXT ROW (WS): With CC, k across.

NEXT ROW (RS): With CC, k1, kfb, k to end (102 st).

NEXT ROW (WS): With MC, k across.

NEXT ROW (RS): With MC, k1, kfb, k to end (103 st).

NEXT ROW (WS): With MC, k across.

NEXT ROW (RS): With MC, k1, kfb, k to end (104 st).

NEXT ROW (WS): With CC, k across.

NEXT ROW (RS): With CC, k1, kfb, k to end (105 st).

NEXT ROW (WS): With CC, k across.

NEXT ROW (RS): With CC, k1, kfb, k to end (106 st).

NEXT ROW (WS): With MC, k across.

NEXT ROW (RS): With MC, k1, kfb, k to end (107 st).

NEXT ROW (WS): With MC, k across.

NEXT ROW (RS): With MC, k1, kfb, k to end (108 st).

NEXT ROW (WS): With CC, k across.

NEXT ROW (RS): With CC, k1, kfb, k to end (109 st).

NEXT ROW (WS): With CC, k across.

NEXT ROW (RS): With CC, k1, kfb, k to end (110 st).

NEXT ROW (WS): With MC, k across.

NEXT ROW (RS): With MC, k1, kfb, k to end (111 st).

NEXT ROW (WS): With MC, k across.

NEXT ROW (RS): With MC, k1, kfb, k to end (112 st).

NEXT ROW (WS): With CC, k3, p to end.

NEXT ROW (RS): With CC, k1, kfb, k1, [(k2tog) 3 times, (yo, k1) 5 times, yo, (ssk) 3 times] rep bet brackets 4 times more, k to end (113 st).

NEXT ROW (WS): With CC, k3, p to end.

NEXT ROW (RS): With CC, k1, kfb, k to end (114 st).

NEXT ROW (WS): With MC, k3, p to end.

NEXT ROW (RS): With MC, k1, kfb, k1, [(k2tog) 3 times, (yo, k1) 5 times, yo, (ssk) 3 times] rep bet brackets 4 times more, k to end (115 st).

NEXT ROW (WS): With MC, k3, p to end.

NEXT ROW (RS): With MC, k1, kfb, k to end (116 st).

NEXT ROW (WS): With CC, k3, p to end.

NEXT ROW (RS): With CC, k1, kfb, k1, [(k2tog) 3 times, (yo, k1) 5 times, yo, (ssk) 3 times] rep bet brackets 4 times more, k to end (117 st).

NEXT ROW (WS): With CC, k3, p to end.

NEXT ROW (RS): With CC, k1, kfb, k to end (118 st).

NEXT ROW (WS): With MC, k across.

NEXT ROW (RS): With MC, k1, kfb, k to end (119 st).

NEXT ROW (WS): With MC, k across.

NEXT ROW (RS): With MC, k1, kfb, k to end (120 st).

NEXT ROW (WS): With CC, k across.

NEXT ROW (RS): With CC, k1, kfb, k to end (121 st).

NEXT ROW (WS): With CC, k across.

NEXT ROW (RS): With CC, k1, kfb, k to end (122 st).

NEXT ROW (WS): With MC, k across.

NEXT ROW (RS): With MC, k1, kfb, k to end (123 st).

NEXT ROW (WS): With MC, k across.

NEXT ROW (RS): With MC, k1, kfb, k to end (124 st).

NEXT ROW (WS): With CC, k across.

NEXT ROW (RS): With CC, k1, kfb, k to end (125 st).

NEXT ROW (WS): With CC, k across.

NEXT ROW (RS): With CC, k1, kfb, k to end (126 st).

NEXT ROW (WS): With MC, k across.

NEXT ROW (RS): With MC, k1, kfb, k to end (127 st).

NEXT ROW (WS): With MC, k across.

NEXT ROW (RS): With MC, k1, kfb, k to end (128 st).

NEXT ROW (WS): With CC, k across.

NEXT ROW (RS): With CC, k1, kfb, k to end (129 st).

NEXT ROW (WS): With CC, k across.

NEXT ROW (RS): With CC, k1, kfb, k to end (130 st).

NEXT ROW (WS): With MC, k across.

NEXT ROW (RS): With MC, k1, kfb, k to end (131 st).

NEXT ROW (WS): With MC, k across.

NEXT ROW (RS): With MC, k1, kfb, k to end (132 st).

NEXT ROW (WS): With CC, k across.

NEXT ROW (RS): With CC, k1, kfb, k to end (133 st).

NEXT ROW (WS): With CC, k across.

NEXT ROW (RS): With CC, k1, kfb, k to end (134 st).

NEXT ROW (WS): With MC, k3, p to end.

NEXT ROW (RS): With MC, k1, kfb, k1, [(k2tog) 3 times, (yo, k1) 5 times, yo, (ssk) 3 times] rep bet brackets 5 times more, k to end (135 st).

NEXT ROW (WS): With MC, k3, p to end.

NEXT ROW (RS): With MC, k1, kfb, k to end (136 st).

NEXT ROW (WS): With CC, k3, p to end.

NEXT ROW (RS): With CC, k1, kfb, k1, [(k2tog) 3 times, (yo, k1) 5 times, yo, (ssk) 3 times] rep bet brackets 5 times more, k to end (137 st).

NEXT ROW (WS): With CC, k3, p to end.

NEXT ROW (RS): With CC, k1, kfb, k to end (138 st).

NEXT ROW (WS): With MC, k3, p to end.

NEXT ROW (RS): With MC, k1, kfb, k1, [(k2tog) 3 times, (yo, k1) 5 times, yo, (ssk) 3 times] rep bet brackets 5 times more, k to end (139 st).

NEXT ROW (WS): With MC, k3, p to end.

NEXT ROW (RS): With MC, k1, kfb, k to end (140 st).

NEXT ROW (WS): With CC, k3, p to end.

NEXT ROW (RS): With CC, k1, kfb, k1, [(k2tog) 3 times, (yo, k1) 5 times, yo, (ssk) 3 times] rep bet brackets 5 times more, k to end (141 st).

NEXT ROW (WS): With CC, k3, p to end.

NEXT ROW (RS): With CC, k1, kfb, k to end (142 st).

NEXT ROW (WS): With MC, k to end.

NEXT ROW (RS): With MC, k1, kfb, k to end (143 st).

REP these 2 rows until you have worked 2" (5 cm) of garter st. BO with medium loose tension on the next row.

WEAVE IN ends and wet block flat, drawing out the points of the shawl to best show the pattern and pinning the edges flat and smooth. Let dry.

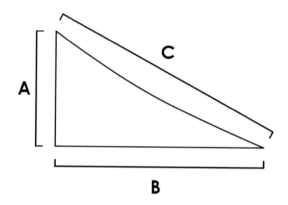

FINISHED MEASUREMENTS

A: 38" (97 cm) long

B: 48" (122 cm) wide

C: 55" (140 cm)

Berry Patch Shawlette

Berries and red blooms remind me of cheerful love notes after a long grey winter (and don't we all need a little color now and then?). Like an ode to the warm season, Berry Patch is a medium-weight, crescent-shape shawlette with tiny knots that mimic ripe berries, feather and fan "trellises" and garter stitch. It's the perfect small accessory to spice up a summer evening.

TIMELINE

With a variety of textures to keep the project interesting, plan on a few hours of knitting each day. With a goal of knitting through approximately ½ a skein (or a little more than 100 yards [91 m]) of yarn per day, an eager knitter can finish Berry Patch in 4 to 5 days.

CONSTRUCTION

Knit from the top center of the crescent with increases at the edges on both the right and wrong side rows, Berry Patch grows side to side, resulting in a long, narrow shawlette with a rounded crescent center.

SKILL LEVEL

Advanced Beginner

SIZE

One size fits most (see schematic for finished measurements)

MATERIALS

Yarn	• Worsted weight | Lolodidit Simple Worsted | 100% superwash Merino | 218 yards (199 m) per 100 g skein | 2 skeins or 436 yards (398 m) total • Color: Sriracha • Yarn substitutions may create different results. Please keep this in mind.
Needles	• U.S. size 9/5.5 mm (32" [80 cm]) circular needle (or size to obtain gauge)
Gauge	• 16 st and 20 rows = 4" (10 cm) in stockinette stitch, blocked
Notions	• Stitch markers, including a locking marker • Darning needle to weave in ends

STITCH GLOSSARY

[ ]	brackets always indicate a repeat
bet	between
BO	bind off
CO	cast on
dec	decrease
inc	increase
k	knit
k2togtbl	knit 2 st together through the back loop (dec 1)
ktbl	knit through the back loop (this will close up the yo from the previous row)
k-yo-k	knit, yarn over, then knit again into the same st (2 st inc)
m	marker
make knot	p 3 st together, leaving them on the left needle—k them together, then p them together again, slipping st off the needle (no st inc or dec)
p	purl
pLm	place locking marker so you can remove it before you reach it
pm	place marker
rep	repeat
RS	right side
sm	slip marker
WS	wrong side
yo	yarn over (inc 1)

BERRY PATCH SHAWLETTE PATTERN

With U.S. size 9/5.5 mm (32" [80 cm]) circular needle, CO 3 st using the cable cast-on method. Note: The cable cast-on method starts your work on the right side immediately.

ROW 1 (RS): [K-yo-k] 3 times (9 st).

ROW 2 (WS): P1, yo, p to last st, yo, p1 (11 st).

ROW 3 (RS): K1, ktbl, k-yo-k, k5, k-yo-k, ktbl, k1 (15 st).

ROW 4 (WS): P1, yo, p to last st, yo, p1 (17 st).

ROW 5 (RS): K1, ktbl, k-yo-k, k to last 3 st, k-yo-k, ktbl, k1 (21 st).

ROW 6 (WS): Rep row 4 (23 st).

ROW 7 (RS): Rep row 5 (27 st).

ROW 8 (WS): Rep row 4 (29 st).

ROW 9 (RS): Rep row 5 (33 st).

ROW 10 (WS): Rep row 4 (35 st).

ROW 11 (RS): Rep row 5 (39 st).

ROW 12 (WS): Rep row 4 (41 st).

ROW 13 (RS): Rep row 5 (45 st).

ROW 14 (WS): Rep row 4 (47 st).

ROW 15 (RS): Rep row 5 (51 st).

ROW 16 (WS): Rep row 4 (53 st).

ROW 17 (RS): Rep row 5 (57 st).

ROW 18 (WS): Rep row 4 (59 st).

ROW 19 (RS): Rep row 5 (63 st).

ROW 20 (WS): Rep row 4 (65 st).

BERRIES BEGIN

ROW 21 (RS): K1, ktbl, k-yo-k, pLm, k1, [make knot, k3] to last 7 st, make knot, k1, pLm, k-yo-k, ktbl, k1 (69 st).

ROW 22 (WS): P1, yo, p to last st, yo, p1 (71 st).

ROW 23 (RS): K1, ktbl, k-yo-k, k to last 3 st, k-yo-k, ktbl, k1 (75 st).

ROW 24 (WS): P1, yo, p to last st, yo, p1 (77 st).

ROW 25 (RS): K1, ktbl, k-yo-k, k to 2 st before m, pm and rem the next marker before you get to it so you can work the next st, [make knot, k3] to 1 st before m, rem the next marker before you get to it so you can work the next st, make knot, k to last 3 st, k-yo-k, ktbl, k1 (81 st).

ROW 26 (WS): P1, yo, p to last st, yo, p1 (83 st).

ROW 27 (RS): K1, ktbl, k-yo-k, k to last 3 st, k-yo-k, ktbl, k1 (87 st).

ROW 28 (WS): P1, yo, p to last st, yo, p1 (89 st).

ROW 29 (RS): K1, ktbl, k-yo-k, k1, [make knot, k3] to last 7 st, make knot, k1, k-yo-k, ktbl, k1 (93 st).

ROW 30 (WS): P1, yo, p to last st, yo, p1 (95 st).

ROW 31 (RS): K1, ktbl, k-yo-k, k to last 3 st, k-yo-k, ktbl, k1 (99 st).

ROW 32 (WS): P1, yo, p to last st, yo, p1 (101 st).

ROW 33 (RS): K1, ktbl, k-yo-k, k to last 3 st, k-yo-k, ktbl, k1 (105 st).

ROW 34 (WS): P1, yo, p to last st, yo, p1 (107 st).

GARTER ROWS

ROW 35 (RS): K1, ktbl, k-yo-k, k to last 3 st, k-yo-k, ktbl, k1 (111 st).

ROW 36 (WS): P1, yo, k to last st, yo, p1 (113 st).

ROW 37 (RS): K1, ktbl, k-yo-k, k to last 3 st, k-yo-k, ktbl, k1 (117 st).

ROW 38 (WS): P1, yo, k to last st, yo, p1 (119 st).

ROW 39 (RS): K1, ktbl, k-yo-k, k to last 3 st, k-yo-k, ktbl, k1 (123 st).

ROW 40 (WS): P1, yo, k to last st, yo, p1 (125 st).

ROW 50 (WS): P1, yo, k to last st, yo, p1 (155 st).

ROW 51 (RS): K1, ktbl, k-yo-k, k to last 3 st, k-yo-k, ktbl, k1 (159 st).

ROW 52 (WS): P1, yo, k to last st, yo, p1 (161 st).

ROW 53 (RS): K1, ktbl, k-yo-k, k to last 3 st, k-yo-k, ktbl, k1 (165 st).

ROW 54 (WS): P1, yo, p to last st, yo, p1 (167 st).

BERRY ROWS

ROW 55 (RS): K1, ktbl, k-yo-k, pLm, k1, [make knot, k3] to last 7 st, make knot, k1, pLm, k-yo-k, ktbl, k1 (171 st).

ROW 56 (WS): P1, yo, p to last st, yo, p1 (173 st).

ROW 57 (RS): K1, ktbl, k-yo-k, k to last 3 st, k-yo-k, ktbl, k1 (177 st).

ROW 58 (WS): P1, yo, p to last st, yo, p1 (179 st).

ROW 59 (RS): K1, ktbl, k-yo-k, k to 2 st before m, rem the next marker before you get to it so you can work the next st, [make knot, k3] to 1 st before m, rem the next marker before you get to it so you can work the next st, make knot, k to last 3 st, k-yo-k, ktbl, k1 (183 st).

ROW 60 (WS): P1, yo, p to last st, yo, p1 (185 st).

ROW 61 (RS): K1, ktbl, k-yo-k, k to last 3 st, k-yo-k, ktbl, k1 (189 st).

ROW 62 (WS): P1, yo, p to last st, yo, p1 (191 st)—remove markers as you work this row.

ROW 63 (RS): K1, ktbl, k-yo-k, k1, [make knot, k3] to last 7 st, make knot, k1, k-yo-k, ktbl, k1 (195 st).

ROW 64 (WS): P1, yo, p to last st, yo, p1 (197 st).

ROW 65 (RS): K1, ktbl, k-yo-k, k to last 3 st, k-yo-k, ktbl, k1 (201 st).

ROW 66 (WS): P1, yo, p to last st, yo, p1 (203 st).

ROW 67 (RS): K1, ktbl, k-yo-k, k to last 3 st, k-yo-k, ktbl, k1 (207 st).

ROW 68 (WS): P1, yo, p to last st, yo, p1 (209 st).

GARTER ROWS

ROW 69 (RS): K1, ktbl, k-yo-k, k to last 3 st, k-yo-k, ktbl, k1 (213 st).

ROW 70 (WS): P1, yo, k to last st, yo, p1 (215 st).

TRELLIS ROWS

ROW 41 (RS): K1, ktbl, k-yo-k, pm, k1 [k2togtbl, k9, k2tog] to last 4 st, k1, pm, k-yo-k, ktbl, k1 (111 st).

ROW 42 (WS): P1, yo, p to last st, yo, p1 (113 st).

ROW 43 (RS): K1, ktbl, k-yo-k, k3, sm, k1, [k2togtbl, k7, k2tog] to 1 st before m, k1, sm, k3, k-yo-k, ktbl, k1 (99 st).

ROW 44 (WS): P1, yo, p to last st, yo, p1 (101 st).

ROW 45 (RS): K1, ktbl, k-yo-k, k6, sm, k1, [k2togtbl, yo, (k1, yo) 5 times, k2tog] to 1 st before m, k1, sm, k6, k-yo-k, ktbl, k1 (141 st).

ROW 46 (WS): P1, yo, p to last st, yo, p1 (143 st)—remove markers as you work this row.

GARTER ROWS

ROW 47 (RS): K1, ktbl, k-yo-k, k to last 3 st, k-yo-k, ktbl, k1 (147 st).

ROW 48 (WS): P1, yo, k to last st, yo, p1 (149 st).

ROW 49 (RS): K1, ktbl, k-yo-k, k to last 3 st, k-yo-k, ktbl, k1 (153 st).

ROW 71 (RS): K1, ktbl, k-yo-k, k to last 3 st, k-yo-k, ktbl, k1 (219 st).

ROW 72 (WS): P1, yo, k to last st, yo, p1 (221 st).

ROW 73 (RS): K1, ktbl, k-yo-k, k to last 3 st, k-yo-k, ktbl, k1 (225 st).

ROW 74 (WS): P1, yo, k to last st, yo, p1 (227 st).

TRELLIS ROWS

ROW 75 (RS): K1, ktbl, k-yo-k, pm, [k2togtbl, k9, k2tog] to last 3 st, pm, k-yo-k, ktbl, k1 (197 st).

ROW 76 (WS): P1, yo, p to last st, yo, p1 (199 st).

ROW 77 (RS): K1, ktbl, k-yo-k, k3, sm, [k2togtbl, k7, k2tog] to m, sm, k3, k-yo-k, ktbl, k1 (169 st).

ROW 78 (WS): P1, yo, p to last st, yo, p1 (171 st).

ROW 79 (RS): K1, ktbl, k-yo-k, k6, sm, [k2togtbl, yo, (k1, yo) 5 times, k2tog] to m, sm, k6, k-yo-k, ktbl, k1 (243 st).

ROW 80 (WS): P1, yo, p to last st, yo, p1 (245 st)—remove markers as you work this row.

GARTER ROWS

ROW 81 (RS): K1, ktbl, k-yo-k, k to last 3 st, k-yo-k, ktbl, k1 (249 st).

ROW 82 (WS): P1, yo, k to last st, yo, p1 (251 st).

ROW 83 (RS): K1, ktbl, k-yo-k, k to last 3 st, k-yo-k, ktbl, k1 (255 st).

ROW 84 (WS): P1, yo, k to last st, yo, p1 (257 st).

ROW 85 (RS): K1, ktbl, k-yo-k, k to last 3 st, k-yo-k, ktbl, k1 (261 st).

ROW 86 (WS): P1, yo, k to last st, yo, p1 (263 st).

STOCKINETTE ROWS

ROW 87 (RS): K1, ktbl, k-yo-k, k to last 3 st, k-yo-k, ktbl, k1 (267 st).

ROW 88 (WS): P1, yo, p to last st, yo, p1 (269 st).

ROW 89 (RS): K1, ktbl, k-yo-k, k to last 3 st, k-yo-k, ktbl, k1 (273 st).

ROW 90 (WS): P1, yo, p to last st, yo, p1 (275 st).

ROW 91 (RS): K1, ktbl, k-yo-k, k to last 3 st, k-yo-k, ktbl, k1 (279 st).

ROW 92 (WS): P1, yo, p to last st, yo, p1 (281 st).

ROW 93 (RS): K1, ktbl, k-yo-k, k to last 3 st, k-yo-k, ktbl, k1 (285 st).

GARTER ROWS

ROW 94 (WS): P1, yo, k to last st, yo, p1 (287 st).

ROW 95 (RS): K1, ktbl, k-yo-k, k to last 3 st, k-yo-k, ktbl, k1 (291 st).

ROW 96 (WS): P1, yo, k to last st, yo, p1 (293 st).

ROW 97 (RS): K1, ktbl, k-yo-k, k to last 3 st, k-yo-k, ktbl, k1 (297 st).

ROW 98 (WS): P1, yo, k to last st, yo, p1 (299 st).

ROW 99 (RS): BO with a stretchy or loose bind-off on this row.

WEAVE IN ends and wet block, pinning the top edge flat along the blocking mat (this will help to "train" the top edge if it happens to seem bowed in an arc while you are knitting it). Once the top section is pinned straight across, flat, draw the remainder of the shawl down and out, pinning it taut on the mat. Let dry.

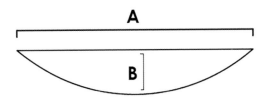

FINISHED MEASUREMENTS

A: 62" (157 cm) tip to tip

B: 13½" (34 cm) top to bottom

Multi-Season Cowls

When you have a single weekend and want almost-instant gratification, there's nothing better than a cowl project (the Darling Bud Cowl on page 131, for example, comes together in no time!). Inspired by designs throughout the book, these cowls are companion projects to their namesake shawls and wraps; they share some of the same sweet details as the larger projects that inspired them, but in bite-size versions that you can knit in an even shorter period of time. Perfect for autumn, winter or spring, you'll find these small projects are suitable to wear most of the year. They're ideal for using up single skeins of stash yarn, too, which can help you turn your stash into quick gifts for loved ones. If you're looking for a small project to take on the go, or to knit for someone who says they're "not a shawl person," cowls are always a good bet.

Sugarplum Cowl

Like its shawl counterpart on page 69, the Sugarplum Cowl is dotted with wooly "plums" that are offset with garter stitch. If you can't get enough of the texture on the shawl, you'll love this quick sidekick piece. On its own, the Sugarplum Cowl is a lovely accessory that you can work up in no time.

TIMELINE

If you're on a deadline, you could work up the Sugarplum Cowl in a single day. It makes for a perfect weekend project!

CONSTRUCTION

Worked flat and seamed together at the end, the pattern easily memorized after a single repeat. (While you could easily join it to work in the round, working it flat means very little purling is required.)

SKILL LEVEL

Intermediate

SIZE

One size fits most (see schematic for finished measurements)

MATERIALS

Yarn	• Worsted weight | Lolodidit Simple Worsted | 100% superwash Merino | 218 yards (199 m) per 100 g skein • Color: Angry Rhino • Yarn substitutions may create different results. Please keep this in mind.
Needles	• U.S. size 9/5.5 mm (16" [40 cm]) circular needle
Gauge	• 17 st and 32 rows = 4" (10 cm) in garter stitch, blocked
Notions	• Darning needle for weaving ends and seaming

STITCH GLOSSARY

[ ]	brackets always indicate a repeat
BO	bind off
CO	cast on
k	knit
k4tog	knit 4 st together (dec 3)
k4togtbl	knit 4 st together through back loop (dec 3)
p	purl
RS	right side
st	stitch/stitches
WS	wrong side
yo	yarn over (inc 1)

SUGARPLUM COWL PATTERN

With U.S. size 9/5.5 mm (16" [40 cm]) circular needle, CO 93 st using the cable cast-on method.

ROWS 1–10: K.

ROW 11 (RS): K2, [yo, k8, yo, k1] to end of row, ending k1.

ROW 12 (WS): K3, [p8, k3] to end of row.

ROW 13 (RS): K3, [yo, k8, yo, k3] to end of row.

ROW 14 (WS): K4, [p8, k5] to end of row, ending k4 instead of k5.

ROW 15 (RS): K4, [yo, k8, yo, k5] to end of row, ending k4 instead of k5.

ROW 16 (WS): K5, [p8, k7] to end of row, ending k5 instead of k7.

ROW 17 (RS): K5, [k4togtbl, k4tog, k7] to end of row, ending k5 instead of k7.

ROWS 18–22: K.

REP rows 11–22, 3 times more (for a total of 4). BO on row 22 as you knit across. Break yarn, leaving a tail (3–4" [7.5–10 cm]) to weave in later.

BRING the sides together and stitch closed using your favorite seaming method.

WEAVE IN ends and wet block flat, turning as needed for even drying.

FINISHED MEASUREMENTS

A: 21" (53 cm) circumference

B: 11½" (29 cm) tall

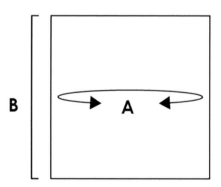

Darling Bud Cowl

If you find yourself with a free weekend and have a single skein of lovely yarn in your knitting stash, you'll enjoy the Darling Bud Cowl. A spin-off from the Darling Bud Wrap (page 109), the cowl version marries a single bud repeat with intermittent ribbing for a slight ruched effect. The repeat is simple and intuitive, making it a perfect on-the-go project.

TIMELINE
Perfect for a weekend project, the Darling Bud Cowl can easily be finished during a single weekend with a few hours of knitting each day.

CONSTRUCTION
Worked in the round with alternating bands of eyelets and ribbing, this project has no defined top or bottom.

SKILL LEVEL
Advanced Beginner

SIZE
One size fits most (see schematic for finished measurements)

MATERIALS

Yarn	• Light worsted weight | Purl Soho Flax Down | 43% baby alpaca, 42% extra fine Merino, 15% linen | 219 yards (200 m) per 100 g skein | 1 skein or 219 yards (200 m) total • Color: Rose Granite • Yarn substitutions may create different results. Please keep this in mind.
Needles	• U.S. size 5/3.75 mm (16" [40 cm]) circular needle • U.S. size 7/4.5 mm (16" [40 cm]) circular needle
Gauge	• 20 st and 30 rows = 4" (10 cm) in Darling Bud pattern, blocked
Notions	• Stitch markers • Darning needle to weave in ends

STITCH GLOSSARY

[ ]	brackets always indicate a repeat
BO	bind off
BOR	beginning of round
CO	cast on
inc	increase
k	knit
p	purl
pm	place marker
rep	repeat
s2kp2	slip 2 st as if to knit, k the next st on the left needle, then pass the 2 slipped st over (dec 2)
st	stitch/stitches
yo	yarn over (inc 1)

DARLING BUD COWL PATTERN

With U.S. size 5/3.75 mm (16" [40 cm]) circular needle, CO 120 st using the cable cast-on method.

SET-UP ROW: [K2, p2] to end of row. Join to work in the round and pm to denote BOR.

ROUNDS 1-12: [K2, p2] to end of round. Transition to a larger needle on the final round (and work the remainder of the cowl with the larger needle until the final ribbing transition).

ROUNDS 13-16: K.

ROUND 17: [Yo, s2kp2, yo, k3] to end.

ROUND 18: K.

ROUND 19: [K1, yo, s2kp2, yo, k2] to end.

ROUND 20: K.

ROUND 21: Rep round 17.

ROUND 22: K.

ROUNDS 23–26: K.

REP rounds 1–26, 2 times more (for a total of 3).

TRANSITION to U.S. size 5 (3.75 mm) needle and work rounds 1–12 once more.

BO on round 12 with medium tension (the edge should not be restrictive—if it is, BO more loosely).

WET BLOCK flat, pinning in place and turning as needed until dry.

FINISHED MEASUREMENTS

A: 24" (60 cm) circumference

B: 12" (30 cm) tall

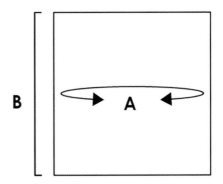

Forager Cowl

When you're looking for an accessory that makes a statement, this cozy cowl might be just the thing. With slipped stitches, garter stitch and cables, the Forager Cowl is a heavily textured project that will keep your interest from start to finish. The pattern incorporates loose strands that are left unworked and then knit into place on later rows, creating the little arrow panels between the cables. If you love texture, the Forager Cowl is for you.

TIMELINE

An easy project for a single weekend, Forager uses just 150 grams of yarn. Work 50 grams (or 1 small skein) per day to finish in 3 days, or speed things up by working 75 grams (or 1½ small skeins) per day. Either way, you'll have a finished piece in no time.

CONSTRUCTION

Forager is cast on at the bottom and worked in one piece (in the round) from bottom to top. Cables and garter ridges (with a slipped stitch pattern) are worked in alternating columns throughout.

SKILL LEVEL

Intermediate

SIZE

One size fits most (see schematic for finished measurements)

MATERIALS

Yarn	• Worsted weight | Blue Sky Woolstok | 100% fine Highland wool | 123 yards (112 m) per 50 g skein | 3 skeins or 369 yards (337 m) total • Color: Grey Harbor • Yarn substitutions may create different results. Please keep this in mind.
Needles	• U.S. size 7/4.5 mm (16" [40 cm]) circular needle
Gauge	• 21 st and 31 rows = 4" (10 cm) in pattern stitch, blocked
Notions	• Stitch markers • Cable needle • Darning needle to weave in ends

STITCH GLOSSARY

[ ]	brackets always indicate a repeat
BO	bind off
BOR	beginning of round
CO	cast on
C8B	cable 8 back (place 4 st on cable needle and hold to back, knit the next 4 st on the left needle, then knit the 4 st from the cable needle) (Optional: see last page for chart)
C8F	cable 8 front (place 4 st on cable needle and hold to front, knit the next 4 st on the left needle, then knit the 4 st from the cable needle (Optional: see last page for chart)
k	knit
kuls	insert right needle under loose strand from sl5wyif, then knit it with the next st on the left needle, tucking the loose strand in with the st
p	purl
pm	place marker
rep	repeat
sl5wyif	slip 5 st to the right needle with yarn in front (do not knit them)—be sure not to pull the yarn tight as you slip the st
sm	slip marker
st	stitch/stitches

FORAGER COWL PATTERN

With U.S. size 7/4.5 mm (16" [40 cm]) circular needle, CO 144 st using the cable cast-on method. Do not join yet.

BOTTOM BORDER

SET-UP ROUND: K across, then join to work in the round and pm to denote BOR.

ROUND 1: P2, [k5, p3] to last st, ending final repeat with p1, instead of p3.

ROUND 2: K2, [sl5wyif, k3] to last st, ending k1, instead of k3.

ROUND 3: Rep round 1.

ROUND 4: K4, [kuls, k7] to end of round.

REP Bottom Border (rounds 1–4) 2 more times (for a total of 3), then work Bottom Border round 1 once more before moving to the Body.

BODY

NOTE: Bold st on both rounds 4 below are also shown on the Cable Chart on the next page.

SECTION 1

ROUND 1: P2, k5, p3, pm, k13, pm, [p3, k5, p3, pm, k13, pm] to last st, skipping the last "pm" and ending p1.

ROUND 2: K2, sl5wyif, k3, sm, k13, [sm, k3, sl5wyif, k3, sm, k13] to last st, ending k1.

ROUND 3: P2, k5, p3, sm, k13, [sm, p3, k5, p3, sm, k13] to last st, ending p1.

ROUND 4: K4, kuls, k5, sm, **C8F**, **k5**, [sm, k5, kuls, k5, sm, **C8F**, **k5**] to last st, ending k1.

SECTION 2

ROUND 1: P2, k5, p3, sm, k13, sm, [p3, k5, p3, sm, k13, sm] to last st, skipping the last "sm" and ending p1.

ROUND 2: K2, sl5wyif, k3, sm, k13, [sm, k3, sl5wyif, k3, sm, k13] to last st, ending k1.

ROUND 3: P2, k5, p3, sm, k13, [sm, p3, k5, p3, sm, k13] to last st, ending p1.

ROUND 4: K4, kuls, k5, sm, **k5**, **C8B**, [sm, k5, kuls, k5, sm, **k5**, **C8B**] to last st, ending k1.

REP Sections 1 and 2 until cowl measures approximately 10–11" (25–27.5 cm) from cast-on edge, ending after completing one full section (either Section 1 or Section 2).

TOP BORDER

ROUND 1: P2, [k5, p3] to last st, ending final repeat with p1 instead of p3.

ROUND 2: K2, [sl5wyif, k3] to last st, ending final repeat with k1, instead of k3.

ROUND 3: Rep round 1.

ROUND 4: K4, [kuls, k7] to end of round, ending k3, kuls.

REP Top Border (rounds 1–4) 2 more times (for a total of 3), then work Top Border round 1 once more. BO with medium tension in knit. Wet block, then pin flat and let dry.

CABLE CHART

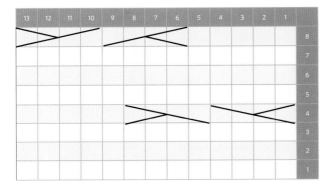

KEY

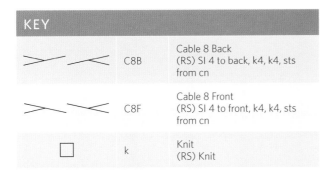

⟩⟨	C8B	Cable 8 Back (RS) Sl 4 to back, k4, k4, sts from cn
⟨⟩	C8F	Cable 8 Front (RS) Sl 4 to front, k4, k4, sts from cn
☐	k	Knit (RS) Knit

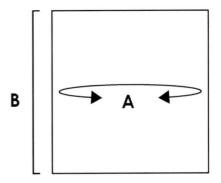

FINISHED MEASUREMENTS

A: 28" (71 cm) circumference

B: 12" (30 cm) tall

Spiced Ginger Cowl

Sometimes I enjoy a stitch pattern so much that I find ways to incorporate it into other projects. Like its shawl counterpart on page 13, the patterning on the Spiced Ginger Cowl is created with a series of simple increases and decreases. The rich, umber twists with flecks of tweed may send you on a hunt for peppery gingerbread cookies before you've finished.

TIMELINE

At a pace of about ½ skein (or about 115 yards [105 m]) per day, you can finish your cowl in 2 to 3 days depending on your pace and available knitting time.

CONSTRUCTION

Cast-on flat and joined to work in the round, the design begins to form quickly and will become easy to follow without a pattern after just a few repeats. In spite of its appearance, the texture pattern is worked with simple increases and decreases (no cables!).

SKILL LEVEL

Advanced Beginner

SIZE

One size fits most (see schematic for finished measurements)

MATERIALS

Yarn	• DK weight | The Farmers Daughter Fibers Craggy Tweed | 85% superwash Merino, 15% NEP (tweedy bits) | 231 yards (211 m) per 100 g skein | 1 skein or 231 yards (211 m) total • Color: Eagle Eye • Yarn substitutions may create different results. Please keep this in mind.
Needles	• U.S. size 8/5 mm (16" [40 cm]) circular needle
Gauge	• 19 st and 26 rows = 4" (10 cm) in pattern stitch, blocked
Notions	• Stitch marker • Darning needle to weave in ends

STITCH GLOSSARY

[ ]	brackets always indicate a repeat
bet	between
BO	bind off
BOR	beginning of round
CO	cast on
dec	decrease
inc	increase
k	knit
p	purl
pm	place marker
rep	repeat
ssk	slip, slip, knit 2 together (dec 1)
st	stitch/stitches
yo	yarn over (inc 1)

SPICED GINGER COWL PATTERN

With U.S. size 8/5 mm (16" [40 cm]) circular needle, and using the cable cast-on method, CO 100 st. Pm to denote BOR and join to work in the round.

SET-UP ROUND: K.

ROUND 1: [P1, yo, k3, ssk, k4] to end of round.

ROUND 2: [P1, k9] to end of round.

ROUND 3: [P1, k1, yo, k3, ssk, k3] to end of round.

ROUND 4: Rep round 2.

ROUND 5: [P1, k2, yo, k3, ssk, k2] to end of round.

ROUND 6: Rep round 2.

ROUND 7: [P1, k3, yo, k3, ssk, k1] to end of round.

ROUND 8: Rep round 2.

ROUND 9: [P1, k4, yo, k3, ssk] to end of round.

ROUNDS 10 AND 11: Rep round 2.

REP rounds 1–11 until you have nearly finished the full skein of yarn, with just a few yards remaining. BO on a row 11 in pattern with medium tension.

VARIATION: If you have time for a larger project (and have extra yarn), try a wider infinity cowl that you can wear doubled by casting on 250 stitches (or any multiple of 10) and working the pattern as written.

WEAVE IN ends and wet block flat, pinning to size.

FINISHED MEASUREMENTS

A: 21" (53 cm) circumference

B: 13" (33 cm) tall

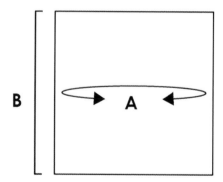

Glacier Cowl

I traveled several times to the Great Lakes area of the United States—right in the middle of a rough winter. While I don't normally need heavy winter gear where I live, it was painfully obvious that winter in that part of the country was an entirely different animal. I can't tell you how much I wished I'd had this cowl with me (or its counterpart, the Glacier Wrap on page 65) to ward off the bone-chilling wind on those icy days. The dense zig-zag fabric of the Glacier Cowl is knit with marled two-tone wool and is just what you'll want for the coldest days of winter.

TIMELINE

Worked with just 2 skeins of aran weight wool and an almost-instantly memorized pattern repeat, most knitters can zip through their Glacier Cowl in just 2 to 3 days.

CONSTRUCTION

Worked in the round with a 4-row repeat, the texture is created with alternating rows of decreases and increases. Be cautious not to count your stitches after round 2 or 4 as you'll naturally lose stitches on those rows due to decreases. Rows 3 and 5, which feature staggered increases, will make up the difference; by the time you end the 4-row repeat, you should be back to your original stitch count.

SKILL LEVEL

Advanced Beginner

SIZE

One size fits most (see schematic for finished measurements)

SIZING TIP

If you have enough yarn for a wider cowl, try casting on a larger number of stitches (any multiple of 12).

MATERIALS

Yarn	• Aran weight | Purl Soho Worsted Twist | 100% Merino wool | 164 yards (150 m) per 100 g skein | 2 skeins or 328 yards (300 m) total
	• Color: Oatmeal Grey
	• Yarn substitutions may create different results. Please keep this in mind.

MATERIALS

Needles	• U.S. size 8/5 mm (24" [60 cm]) circular needle
Gauge	• 24 st and 20 rows = 4" (10 cm) in pattern stitch, blocked
	*Although it seems disproportionate that the row gauge number is smaller than the stitch gauge, this is the natural result of the pattern stitch and is not an error.
Notions	• Stitch marker
	• Darning needle to weave in ends

STITCH GLOSSARY

[ ]	brackets always indicate a repeat
BO	bind off
BOR	beginning of round
CO	cast on
k	knit
p	purl
p1-yo-p1	purl 1, then yo and purl 1 again into the same st (2 st inc)
pm	place marker
rep	repeat
s2kp2	slip 2 st as if to knit, k the next st on the left needle, then pass the 2 slipped st over (dec 2)
st	stitch/stitches
yo	yarn over (inc 1)

GLACIER COWL PATTERN

With U.S. size 8/5 mm (24" [60 cm]) circular needle, CO 120 st using your preferred method. Knit 1 row, then pm and join to work in the round.

ROUND 1: P.

ROUND 2: [K9, s2kp2] to end of round.

ROUND 3: [P4, p1-yo-p1 in next st, p4, k1] to end of round. Remove BOR marker, slip 1 purlwise, replace marker. (This will move the BOR marker 1 st to the left to prepare to work the next round.)

ROUND 4: Rep round 2.

ROUND 5: Rep round 3.

REP rounds 2 through 5 until you have nearly finished the second skein of yarn, ending with round 5. BO on the next round in knit with medium tension.

WEAVE IN ends and wet block flat, allowing to dry completely before wearing.

TIP: After weaving in the ends, wait to trim the excess thread bits that remain until after blocking. This allows the fiber to shift while blocking without tugging the ends out of place. When blocking is complete, trim away any excess yarn that remains from the ends you've woven in.

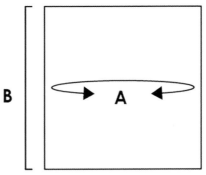

FINISHED MEASUREMENTS

A: 21" (53 cm) circumference

B: 13" (33 cm) tall

Techniques

TIDY EDGES

Smooth, crisp edges can make such a difference in the finished look of a shawl. While working through shawls (or other projects knit flat), be sure to work the first stitch tightly, and as you insert your working needle into the second stitch, give the working yarn an extra tug before you complete the stitch. This will firm up the edge significantly. If you do this at the start of every row—paying special attention to pulling the working yarn tight just before you complete the second stitch—you'll notice an incredible difference in your edges.

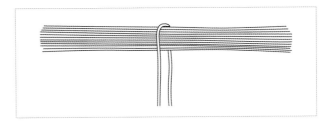
Step 1.1

TASSELS

A tassel can add a little spark to nearly any shawl. If you have enough yarn left over, consider adding one to your next project (such as the Puddlejumper Shawl on page 107). Block your shawl first, and make the tassel while it's drying.

STEP ONE: Cut even lengths of yarn 10" (25 cm) long (how many strands of yarn you'll need is up to you, but I recommend 30-40 strands at a minimum). Fold the strands in half, and use an extra piece of yarn (6-8" [15-20 cm] long) to tie tightly around the very center of the 10" (25 cm) strands, wrapping it around twice, then cinching it tightly closed and tying a small knot. This tie should seal the long strands together at their midpoint. Leave the tails of the extra piece of yarn in place so you can attach the tassel to your project.

STEP TWO: With the strands still folded in half, and using a separate strand of the same yarn (6-8" [15-20 cm] long), measure approximately 1" (2.5 cm) down from the center/top of the tassel and tie the strand around the tassel to create a "bulb" at the top. Wrap the yarn around the tassel 4-5 more times and tie it tightly in place with a knot.

STEP THREE: Use a darning needle to pull the tails down into the body of the tassel. The loose strands at the top of the tassel (from tying it together at the midpoint) can then be used to attach the tassel to the lower center point of your shawl with a simple knot as shown. Use a darning needle to draw the leftover strands down into the body of the tassel where they will become part of the lower tassel strands.

ATTACH the tassel to the bottom center point of a triangle shawl, or create tassels for all four edges of a rectangular wrap.

Step 1.2

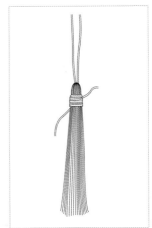

Step 2

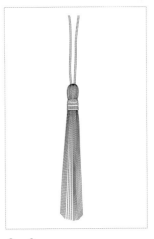
Step 3

PROVISIONAL CAST-ON

A provisional cast-on is a great tool for projects that require the grafting of live stitches when you finish. There are many different methods for creating a provisional cast-on, but my favorite is worked with a crochet hook and waste yarn. It's easy to remove when the time comes, leaving the first row of stitches ready for the next step.

I recommend a metal crochet hook with a narrow neck and pointy top—I've found it to be the easiest to use. A hook that is similar in circumference to your knitting needle will work nicely.

STEP ONE: Begin by making a slip knot with waste yarn on your crochet hook (the amount of waste yarn you'll need will depend on the project, but give yourself ample yarn so you won't run out before you reach the stitch count you need). Lay the hook (with the slip knot attached) directly on top of your knitting needle in perpendicular fashion (it should look like it's making a plus sign), and wrap the working yarn so that it sits underneath the knitting needle.

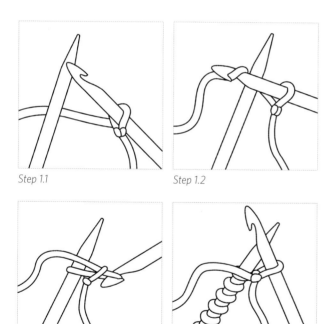

Step 1.1

Step 1.2

Step 2.1

Step 2.2

STEP TWO: Holding the working yarn in your left hand, use the hook in your right hand to grab the working yarn and pull it through the slip knot on the crochet hook. This process will have secured one loop around the knitting needle and will leave you with one stitch on the crochet hook. Move the working yarn around the back of the knitting needle so it sits in its original location, underneath the knitting needle. Once again, hold the working yarn in your left hand and use the hook in your right hand to grab the working yarn and to draw it through the single loop on the hook. Repeat this process until you have the number of stitches needed on your knitting needle.

When you are finished, cut the working yarn and draw the final loop through the last stitch on the hook and let it dangle to the side.

RUSSIAN GRAFTING

This grafting technique is a slick alternative to Kitchener stitch, and although it doesn't create an invisible graft, it works beautifully for grafting live stitches and leaves a decorative "zipper" seam.

You will need a crochet hook slightly smaller than the circumference of the knitting needles you've used for the project—hooks with a tapered neck and pointy top work best for this process.

PREPARATION STEP: Using the same needles you used for your project, slide one needle through the live stitches on the cast-on row so that the tip of the needle is positioned ready to work the right side of the row. As you do this, remove any excess yarn from the provisional cast-on (if applicable). Slide your other needle through the live stitches on the final row of the project, with the working needle ready to work a wrong side row. Place the wrong sides of your knitting together so that the right sides are facing outward and the working tip of both needles are aligned. Your needles should be placed parallel to each other with the tips of the needles pointing to the right. (If you are left-handed, you will work this same process with the needle tips pointing to the left, instead.)

STEP ONE: Hold your needles together in your left hand (or right hand if you are left-handed). Insert the crochet hook through the first stitch on the back needle as if to knit (you will insert the hook into the stitch as if you are working it on the wrong side), then slide it off onto the hook.

STEP TWO: Insert the hook into the first stitch on the front needle (the one closest to you), inserting it through the right side as if to knit. You should now have two stitches on your crochet hook (one from the back needle and one from the front needle).

STEP THREE: With your hook, draw the second (newest) stitch through the first stitch, leaving one stitch left on your hook.

The graft is now set up. Work the remainder of the graft as follows.

Step 1.1

Step 1.2

Step 2

STEP FOUR: As in step one, insert the hook into the first stitch on the back needle (on the wrong side) as if to knit = two stitches on the hook. Slide this new stitch through the first stitch on the hook = one stitch left on the hook. Insert the hook into the first stitch on the front needle (on the right side) as if to knit = two stitches on the hook. Slide this new stitch through the first stitch on the hook = one stitch left on the hook.

Step 3.1

Step 3.2

WORK step four until you've grafted all the stitches from both needles. When you have one stitch left on the hook, draw the yarn left from the previous end of the row through this final stitch and weave it securely in place.

TIP: The grafting method should always be worked by drawing one stitch from the back, then one stitch from the front, and so on. If you ever lose your spot, you can simply count how many stitches are left on both needles and you will know that you are ready to work on the side that has one stitch more than the other needle.

This method works beautifully for grafting live stitches on anything you may be knitting.

Yarn Resources

BLUE SKY FIBERS

www.blueskyfibers.com

BROOKLYN TWEED

www.brooklyntweed.com

LITTLE FOX YARN

www.littlefoxyarn.com

LOLODIDIT

www.lolodidit.com

PURL SOHO

www.purlsoho.com

459 Broome St., New York, NY 10013

SKACEL COLLECTION

(Source for HiKoo & Zitron yarns in this book)

www.skacelknitting.com

Available to consumers at www.makers mercantile.com or other fine yarn retailers

THE FARMERS DAUGHTER FIBERS

www.thefarmersdaughterfibers.com

210 17th St. N, Great Falls, MT 59401

THREE IRISH GIRLS

www.threeirishgirls.com

Acknowledgments

I am forever grateful to the knitters, yarn folks, yarn shop owners and yarn makers (and sheep!) who make this work possible. Many thanks to the companies that provided yarn support: Skacel Collection, Lolodidit, The Farmers Daughter Fibers, Brooklyn Tweed, Purl Soho, Three Irish Girls, Little Fox Yarn and Blue Sky Fibers. Thank you to my team of sample knitters: Brianna Thornton, Cindy Tripp, Cristi Ebersole, Cydney Gordon, Erika Close, Jillian Monier, Lisa Kirk, Nancy Taylor and Tiffany Jenkins. And to my entire team of test knitters: Thank you! You're amazing!

Thank you to my photographer, Belen Mercer, for sticking around to photograph this second book together before she ventured off on her Pacific Crest Trail adventure. Thanks to my in-house artist, Jonah Greene (who also happens to be my son), for providing the schematics and illustrations. Thank you to my tech editor, Cathy Susko, for her ongoing assistance with pattern accuracy. Thank you to Page Street Publishing and to my editor Rebecca Fofonoff for their continued support and partnership.

Most of all, thank you to my husband, Scott—my best pal and staunchest supporter—who has been asking for a new sweater and who might finally get one now that this book is finished.

About the Author

Marie Greene is an independent knitwear designer, instructor and author of the book *Seamless Knit Sweaters in 2 Weeks*. Her innovative approach to knitting has gained notice around the world. Her work has been featured in collections for The Fibre Company, Skacel Collection and *Laine Magazine*. You can find her tutorials, workshops, pattern support and technique classes online at oliveknits.com. *Knit Shawls & Wraps in 1 Week* is her second book. Marie lives in Salem, Oregon, with her husband, Scott, with whom she shares three grown sons.

Index